RV

To

Explore the Wild & Wonderful Alaska & Canada

A Budget Friendly Guide to Visit Alaska & Canada in a RV

By

Robert Nichols

Copyrighted Material

Copyright © 2019 – *Valley Of Joy Publishing Press*

All Rights Reserved.
No part of this publication may be reproduced, stored in a retrieval system or transmitted in any form or by any means, electronic, mechanical, photocopying, recording or otherwise without the proper written consent of the copyright holder, except brief quotations used in a review.

Published by:

Valley Of Joy Publishing Press

Cover & Interior designed

By

Robin Nichols

First Edition

WHAT YOU WILL FIND IN THIS GUIDE

What You Will Find In this Guide..3
Part – 1 7
Exploring Canada..7
Introduction..8
Preparation & Packing the Right Gear 12
   What to Pack 15
   For the RV 16
      For Backcountry Camping..17
   Clothing...20
Alberta 22
   Suggested RV Trip #1 23
      Suggested RV Park-1 in Cochrane 27
      Suggested RV Park-2 in Cochrane 28
      Suggested RV Park-1 in Grand Prairie 31
      Suggested RV Park-2 in Grand Prairie 32
   Suggested RV Trip #2 43
      Suggested RV Park in Valleyview...43
      Suggested RV Park-1 in Whitecourt 45
      Suggested RV Park-2 in Whitecourt 45
      Suggested RV Park in Spring Lake.......................................50
      Suggested RV Park in Stony Plain..51
      Suggested RV Park-1 in Edmonton 52
      Suggested RV Park-2 in Edmonton 53
      Suggested RV Park in Saskatoon...55

  7 Must-See Places Around Winnipeg 56

  Suggested RV Park in Portage La Prairie 59

  Suggested RV Park in St. Francis Xavier 60

  Suggested RV Park in Winnipeg 60

  RV Camping at National Parks in Alberta 61

British Columbia 63

  Suggested RV Trip 65

    Suggested RV Park in Burnaby 66

    Suggested RV Park in Surrey 67

  RV Camping at National Parks in British Columbia 73

Manitoba 76

  Suggested City Visit 78

  RV Camping at National Parks in Manitoba 81

New Brunswick 82

  Suggested RV Trip 83

  RV Camping at National Parks in New Brunswick 85

Newfoundland and Labrador 87

  Suggested RV Trip 88

  RV Camping at National Parks in Newfoundland & Labrador .. 90

Northwest Territories 92

  Suggested RV Trip 93

  RV Camping at National Parks in Northwest Territories 95

Nova Scotia 97

  Suggested RV Trip 98

  RV Camping at National Parks in Nova Scotia 104

Ontario 105

  Suggested RV Trip 106

    Suggested RV Park-1 in Niagara Falls 113

Suggested RV Park-2 in Niagara Falls 114
RV Camping at National Parks in Ontario 116
Prince Edward Island 119
Suggested RV Trip 120
Suggested City Visit 124
RV Camping at National Parks in Prince Edward Island 125
Quebec 126
Suggested RV Trip 127
RV Camping at National Parks in Quebec 138
Saskatchewan 140
Suggested City Visit 141
Suggested RV Park-1 in Saskatoon 143
Suggested RV Park-2 in Saskatoon 144
RV Camping at National Parks in Saskatchewan 145
Yukon 146
Suggested City Visit 147
RV Camping at National Parks in Yukon 149
RV Trip to Alaska 152
Things You Should Know 153
Suggested Alaskan Bucket List 155
Suggested RV Trip 157
Suggested RV Park in Anchorage 160
Suggested RV Park in Kenai 164
Suggested RV Trip 165
Suggested RV Park in Valdez 166
Suggested RV Park in Fairbanks 169
Suggested RV Trip 171
RV Camping at Alaska State Parks 180

- Traveling on a Budget 183
  - Boondocking 183
  - Travel in the summer 184
  - Stock Up When Stopping in Large Towns 185
  - Avoid Using American Dollars in Canada 186
  - Be Careful When Purchasing Food and Water 187
  - Keep Track of Your Spending 188
- Conclusion 189
- Last Word 192
- Helpful Links & Resources 194

PART – 1

EXPLORING CANADA

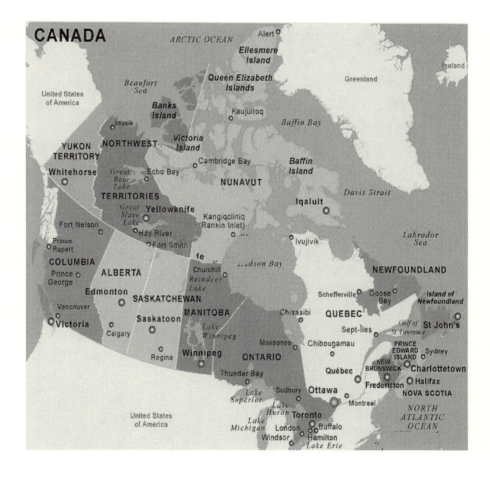

INTRODUCTION

Imagine spending the day hiking a grand forest to reach a view overlooking a lake so crystal clear it mirrors the sky perfectly into a light blue silver sheet spreading on the rocks. Think about the soft sound as small waves trickle onto the sand of the shore. You can almost smell the delicate aroma of algae, fresh grass, and dampened earth.

Once you have imprinted the memory in your mind, you may not want to go back all the way down the trail toward your car and drive away, as that would mean the end of your trip. Yet, your stomach is growling, you are already running low on water, and it is getting colder as the sun sets across the horizon. There is no other choice; you just have to get in the car and drive to stay in a room somewhere away from all the wonders you just witnessed. But what if I told you that is not, in fact, the only option?

What if I told you there was a way to extend your trip with triple the supplies you can carry with you, and wake up every day at a new paradise? Whether it is a forest, beach, buzzing city, or picturesque town, you would get to see as much as you want with the help of a guide, a map, and an RV (recreational vehicle or campervan).

Think of an RV as a more convenient, motorized camping tent. It grants you more room to pack extra supplies, a guaranteed place to sleep, eat, and rest, as well as a warm meal every night in the comfort of a bed. It protects you from sudden harsh weather, takes to safety faster in case of an injury, and allows you to plan your trip at your own pace without rushing out for more food or water.

You only need to park your RV, gather everything you need for your hike or camping trip at that chosen destination, then walk back into the vehicle and refuel while you are on your way to the next adventure. Now, if you or one of your companions has certain difficulties, traveling in an RV is a great alternative to keep exploring the world while being mindful of the health-conscious aspect of things

Of course, RVs have their inconvenient downsides, such as the initial cost of owning or renting one, finding a place to park in, general maintenance, and finding a gas station from time to time. While the prices may be steep, they are worthwhile after considering all the lifelong benefits.

However, if you do not intend on making heavy use of the RV every year, you could always either sell the one you purchased, borrow one from a trusted friend, or rent one for a lower price and a defined period of time. Regardless of which method you choose, dedicating a vacation to venturing into the unknown in a campervan is an absolutely priceless experience, as you will find.

If you have already read my previous book "RV life on a Budget", then I appreciate the support. If you have yet to do so and this is your first guide from me, I hope it is written to your satisfaction and sparks your interest in planning a thorough trip in the northern lands of Canada and Alaska. Let's dive right into the snowy mountains.

PREPARATION & PACKING THE RIGHT GEAR

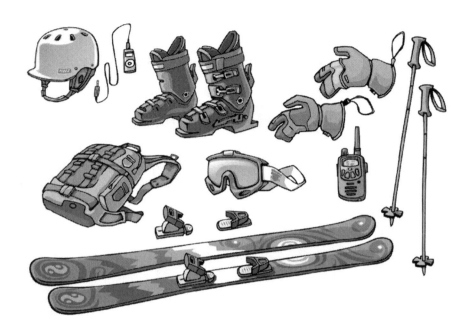

As of this moment, a U.S. citizen may enter Canada with only a valid passport and a birth certificate for anyone under the age of 16. Non-US citizens will typically have to file an eTA (electronic travel authorization) found in the Canada Border Services Agency's website. It is always a tip to regularly check in with the CBSA's website just to make sure the laws do not change at the last minute before your trip.

Most goods are allowed across the border, and since taxes are generally higher in Canada, it can be a good idea to stock up on groceries before your trip. Also, come prepared for higher gas prices. The Canadian Food Inspection Agency oversees pets traveling into the country, and generally, there are no issues as long as your pet has the necessary documents and updated vaccines.

When it comes to your RV make sure you have valid tags, your registration, and insurance information organized neatly in a single place. If you are renting an RV, you must have a copy of the rental contract or a notarized letter authorizing travel into Canada. While your U.S. driver's license is valid, you should be aware of the different laws in the provinces where you're traveling.

For example: in Quebec, all traffic signs are in French. If you intend to visit the French-speaking sections of Canada, you could always make the time for a few free French lessons on Duolingo, just to get the basics in without much trouble.

The campgrounds in Canada will have amenities similar to those in the United States, thankfully enough. Some national and provincial parks have full hookups and showers, while others don't.

You'll also be able to choose from a range of private campgrounds that offer various amenities such as playgrounds and swimming pools for those traveling with children. The main difference is that open campground seasons are shorter since the warm season tends to be shorter itself. Just make sure you get your reservations in advance, and you should be fine.

When it comes to money and banking in Canada, there are some important things to know. Canada doesn't have any pennies and prices are approximated to the nickel. Most places will accept the US dollar, but they will often be taken at par, which isn't ideal since the US dollar is higher in value than the Canadian one.

It is best to exchange your money at a bank or use your credit or debit card for the day's exchange rate. Notify the bank affiliated to your credit cards that you are traveling, so they don't put a last-minute freeze on your accounts. Trust me that is never a fun experience, especially when it is late at night or a Sunday when most banks are already closed, and you are trying to pay for something like dinner at a restaurant.

Now that you know what to expect when traveling north of the border, there is one other thing you need to do to make sure you are ready to travel. We need to discuss what you need to pack for a trip to Canada and Alaska, so you are not traveling too light, but you are also not like Mrs. Potato Head and carrying the strangest items just in case they might be needed.

What to Pack

Traveling by RV to Canada or Alaska means you are adventurous and want to get close to nature with your own terms and comfort. So, for this kind of lifestyle choice you need to be extra prepared, so you don't get stuck out in the wilderness with no means of communication, navigation, or sustenance.

We want to avoid something like that since they are rather traumatizing experiences that may put you off from future trips of that sort. Let's take a look at what is needed for your travels north of the border.

FOR THE RV

If your trip is going to stay on paved roads then you won't need anything other than what you pack on a standard RV trip, which includes items such as non-perishable foods, maps, and guides, an emergency kit, clothes, miscellaneous equipment such as a camera or a fishing rod, sunblock, blankets, a tent, a sleeping bag, and a hefty supply of water.

However, if you plan to head out into the wilderness on gravel or dirt roads, you'll need to pack a few extra things. For example, if you are towing a vehicle, you will need to get a rock guard or thick pad. You may also want to get protection for your headlights, as well as tire chains in case of snow and ice and a tire pressure monitoring system, so you are not stranded in the middle of nowhere with a couple of flat tires.

If you are going to stay off the grid for any amount of time, you should carry extra batteries or consider installing a solar-based system on your RV. Another option is to purchase a solar-powered rechargeable battery, which comes in handy regardless of the situation. Before traveling it is extremely important you check your insurance policy to ensure it is honored in Canada, has extra coverage for your windshield, and that it can tow you as far as 100 miles. Preemptive measures make for a safe trip.

FOR BACKCOUNTRY CAMPING

If you plan to stay anywhere other than frontcountry developed campgrounds, you should make sure you pack a few extra supplies fitting toward the activities you intend to partake in once you reach your chosen destination. Check all your tanks are full and you have plenty of water. For emergencies, make sure you have a shovel, reflective triangles, and cones.

If you have little to no idea about what essentials to bring with you, I have created an outline with the basics of what is needed for any RV trip:

- Maps and Road Guides
- Portable Lights
- Rechargeable Batteries and their Charger
- Camping Tent
- Sleeping Bags
- Bottled Water Supply
- First-Aid Kits
- Matches or Lighters (Lighter Fluid As Well)
- Kitchenware (Cups, Plates, Bowls, Forks, Spoons, Knives, Spatula, Cooking Pots and Pans)
- Cooking Oil
- Napkins
- Can and Bottle Openers
- Rain Jackets and Rain Boots
- Umbrellas
- Sunscreen or Coconut Oil
- Toilet Paper Rolls
- Toiletries (Toothbrushes and Toothpaste, Deodorant, Razor Blades, Nail Clippers, etc.)
- Shower Toiletries (Soap and Hair Shampoo, Sponges)
- Towels
- Trash Bags
- Backpacks

- Old Newspapers
- Backup Fireplace Logs
- Bedding and Pillows
- Laundry Supplies (Quarters, Detergent, Fabric Softener, Cloth Bag)
- Hiking Boots

More miscellaneous supplies include:

- Entertainment - Board Games, Movies, or Books
- Fishing Rods
- Picnic Blankets
- Canoes or Kayaks (and their Paddles)
- Surfboards
- Mountain Bikes
- More Elaborate Kitchenware (Measuring Cups or Spoons, Tea Kettles, Blenders, Tongs, Whisks)
- Binoculars
- Camera Equipment
- Drawing or Painting Supplies
- Pet Leashes and Food (If You Are Bringing Your Furry Companion With You)

CLOTHING

The weather will depend on where in the northern reaches you are. In general, the farther north you travel, the less warm days you'll experience. Expect summer daytime temperatures to range from 55 to 70 degrees Fahrenheit; sometimes it will get warmer on the days that stretch to 18 hours or longer. In the far north, temperatures can be below freezing both day and night.

Since the weather is so unpredictable, it is best to wear layers regardless of which region you visit. No matter what time of the year you are traveling, pack long-sleeved shirts, a hat, proper winter hiking boots, and gloves. In the summer, a jacket or windbreaker is usually enough to keep you warm without turning into too much, while in the winter you'll want to bring a heavy coat and an extra couple of thick sweaters.

If you intend to go hiking, you'll want to pack wool socks and hiking boots, so your feet do not feel like they are about to fall off from the cold.

It may sound funny, but there are instances where your limbs are so exposed to colder weather that they actually begin to freeze, so you want to be as cautious as possible when it comes to your feet. If you choose to travel during the late summer, packing rain gear is essential, and do include a pair of shorts and shirts in case the region you are visiting happen to be warmer than anticipated.

So, that's what you need to know to get started. Now let's start taking a look at what's out there so you can plan your ideal RV trip to Canada and Alaska. I'm going to give you a general overview of each province covered here, as well as a couple, suggested trip itineraries, recommended RV parks, and camping locations.

There are dozens of camping choices in Canada, so I'm going to only talk about camping at national and provincial parks for the sake of time and efficiency. For a complete listing of private campgrounds check out www.camping-canada.com

ALBERTA

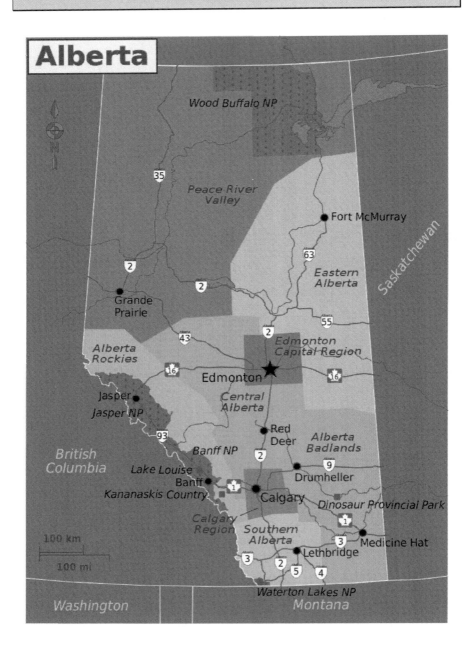

Alberta is a province filled with rugged natural beauty. It is the only place you can go in North America to view a prairie, a boreal forest, and mountains all in one place. Due to this vast ecosystem, Alberta is home to 300 species of birds, 90 mammals, 50 fish, and over 1,700 plants. When it comes to weather, Alberta has more sunny days than all other provinces in Canada. It features low humidity but has a vast contrast in temperature between seasons. In July, the average is 59 to 73 degrees Fahrenheit. In January, the average is negative 7 to 13 degrees Fahrenheit. Despite these extreme numbers, this region is still home to the most comfortable weather in the country.

There are two unique trips you can take to explore this beautiful province and the nearby areas.

SUGGESTED RV TRIP #1

The first suggested trip begins in Lethbridge and involves traveling 2,176 miles to Fairbanks, Alaska. Along this 17+ hour drive, you'll cover three provinces and two countries.

Start in the small prairie town of Lethbridge, where it is sunny 320 days of the year. There are plenty of hiking opportunities in this area with plenty of trails across glacier-carved river valleys. If you wish to take a break from hiking and are more interested in checking out the town itself, you could make a visit to the exotic, serene Nikka Yuko Japanese Garden, first opened back in 1966.

Other worthwhile attractions consist of going for a picnic at the Henderson Lake, catching a show at the New West Theatre, horseback riding in the extensive trails of Pavan Park, or learning about the history of southern Alberta in the largest museum south of Calgary, the Galt Museum & Archives. You will quickly find an activity for all types of preferences in Lethbridge to get you excited for the remainder of the journey.

From here you would go on a 132-mile drive to Calgary, which takes about two hours in total with the regular periodic traffic. This larger city offers you hundreds more of cultural attractions to visit, with the Olympic Park and Calgary Tower being the most popular. If you are visiting in July, be sure to catch the Calgary Stampede, a unique rodeo experience.

Give yourself time to visit this ten-day festival or the nearby Jasper National Park by staying in a nearby park or campground. For the sake of giving you options, here is a quick list to give you brainstorming ideas of where you'd like to go:

- The Lougheed House - Built back in 1891, and now standing as a historic site, you can check out the 14,000 square foot mansion and its beautiful gardens, self-guided tours, and perhaps concerts or art exhibits depending on the month you visit in.

- Glenbow Museum - There is always a museum lover in the group if you are not one yourself. The Glenbow Museum is just the place for such an individual. It has a growing collection of Western Canadian art, as well as a rich background for its culture.

- The Wonderland Sculpture - Almost 40 feet in height, this sculpture was made from bent wire and stands in front of The Bow, a landmark building in the heart of downtown Calgary.

- The Calgary Public Library - For a more quiet setting but still as grand as anything, the Calgary Library has over 1,689,315 books you can choose from, as well as an extensive array of books, audiobooks, and DVDs.
- Downtown Calgary - Restaurants, antique shops, galleries, breweries, oh my! Downtown Calgary is the best place to just relax for the evening and sightsee in a more urban setting.

- The Calgary Zoo - For the little ones in your trip as well as yourself, admission costs $29.95 per adult, $27.95 for seniors, $19.95 for children younger than 15 years of age, and infants of two years and under have free entry. The gates open at 9 am and close at 5 pm, so remember to plan your visit accordingly to that schedule. As for the animals themselves, the zoo has everything from giant pandas, tigers, bears, giraffes, hippos, lemurs, and cranes to gorillas, wild horses, exotic jungle frogs, Komodo Dragons, and tortoises just to name a few. Check at calgaryzoo.com for any fun events to participate in with your loved ones.

- Hammerhead Scenic Tours - If you prefer more of a rural, outdoors adventure rather than one surrounded by people, you can always opt for a full-day, half-day, or multi-day guided tour across Banff National Park, Lake Louise, the Drumheller Badlands, and Waterton National Park, among many more. Alternatively, you could also create your own tour depending on which places you are the most interested in.

- Fish Creek Provincial Park - Nothing like relaxing on a small boat with your trusty fishing rod, with little to no sounds other than birds singing and the occasional splash of fish from the surface of the water. This park is the second largest urban park in the entire country, preceding Rouge National Urban Park in Toronto.

SUGGESTED RV PARK-1 IN COCHRANE

In the town of Cochrane, you'll find Bow RiversEdge Campground. It is open April 1st to October 31st with an average cost of $45 to $50. Pets are welcome with some restrictions and an extra cost.

There is a total of 144 sites with the following amenities:

- ☐ Internet
- ☐ Laundry
- ☐ Ice
- ☐ Restrooms
- ☐ RV Service
- ☐ Showers
- ☐ RV Supplies
- ☐ Recreational Hall
- ☐ Playground
- ☐ Horseshoes

SUGGESTED RV PARK-2 IN COCHRANE

Another option in Cochrane is to stay at the Spring Hill RV Park. This park is open all year with an average cost of $40 to $50 per night. You may be accompanied by your pets, and there is a total of 115 sites with the following amenities:

- ☐ Internet
- ☐ Laundry
- ☐ Metered Gas

- ☐ Groceries
- ☐ Restrooms
- ☐ Showers
- ☐ ATM Machines
- ☐ Ice
- ☐ RV Supplies
- ☐ Snack Bar
- ☐ Playground

From Calgary, it is 189 miles and about three hours to Jasper National Park, which places you in the heart of the Canadian Rockies. There is plenty of nature to explore as well as several nearby small towns. A unique experience is the Jasper Sky tram that offers beautiful views of six mountain ranges, pristine lakes, and long-winding rivers as you travel to the top of Whistlers Mountain.

For animal lovers, you have the chance to spot elk, moose, bighorn sheep, and grizzly bears. However, I would not recommend the sky tram for anyone with vertigo, or a general fear of heights unless they are willing to push their own boundaries.

The next leg of your trip takes you 313 miles and about five hours north to Grande Prairie, incorporated back in 1958. This is a small city that first became a settlement back in the late 1800s, with it originally being occupied by Native Americans who regularly traded with the North West Company. When large oil and natural gas deposits were discovered during the 1950s, a boom of money and prosperity began to take place, along with the creation of pulp mills.

In other words, by the 21st century, Grand Prairie became one of the fastest-growing Canadian cities, according to the Canadian Encyclopedia. Here you can visit the Philip J. Currie Dinosaur Museum for a journey to the past when giant creatures roamed the earth.

Not to mention, during the summer, you can view the trumpeter swans returning to their nesting sites. If you are lucky enough, perhaps you will be able to use a pair of binoculars to catch a glimpse of a few ducklings waddling away behind their mother.

I most certainly do not recommend actually approaching any of the ducklings or the nests, as swans, in particular, are known for being violent, much more so when there is a strange creature in its territory. Remember: one hit from the wing of a swan can break your arm, so definitely do not push it, and respect nature to the best of your ability.

SUGGESTED RV PARK-1 IN GRAND PRAIRIE

At Grand Prairie, you can choose to stay at Camp Tamarack RV Park. This park is open April 15th to October 15th with an average rate of $42 to $49. It is a pet-friendly park. There is a total of 89 sites with the following amenities:

- ☐ Internet
- ☐ RV Supplies
- ☐ Groceries
- ☐ Metered Gas
- ☐ RV Service
- ☐ Restrooms
- ☐ Showers
- ☐ Laundry
- ☐ Ice

- ☐ Horseshoes
- ☐ Playground

SUGGESTED RV PARK-2 IN GRAND PRAIRIE

Another option at Grand Prairie is Country Roads RV Park. This park is open all year with average rates of $46 to $51 per year. It is pet-friendly with some restrictions on breed and quantity. There are 115 sites with the following amenities:

- ☐ Internet
- ☐ Laundry
- ☐ Metered Gas
- ☐ RV Service
- ☐ Restrooms
- ☐ Showers
- ☐ ATM Machines
- ☐ Ice
- ☐ RV Supplies
- ☐ Groceries
- ☐ Self-Service RV Wash
- ☐ Game Room
- ☐ Horseshoes
- ☐ Playground

☐ Recreational Hall

The following chapter in your journey across Canada is about an hour and a half or 81 miles north at Dawson Creek. Along the way, you cross the border into British Columbia. This town marks the start of the iconic Alaska Highway, covering approximately 1,300 miles of scenic landscapes.

The highway was built in just eight months with the sweat and work of approximately 11,000 soldiers and 16,000 Canadian and American civilians at a rate of eight miles of road every day. You can learn the history of this highway at the Alaska Highway House in downtown Dawson Creek. You should also stop by the Mile 0 Park where you can visit the Black Creek Pioneer Village; a living museum that takes you into the past of rural Ontario during the 19th century.

Stretch your legs as much as you can at that previous stop, since we will be facing 600 miles north with a long drive of almost 12 hours in continuation, so be prepared for a long drive or plan somewhere to stop and spend the night. While there are plenty of outdoor hiking and recreational opportunities down this route, the most popular roadside attraction is the Sign Post Forest, originally started in 1942 by a soldier named Carl K. Lindley who was working on the Alaskan Highway.

Nowadays, the Sign Post Forest has grown to over 85,000 signposts that point to destinations throughout the world. You could bring one from your hometown, or have it custom made at the Visitor Information Centre during your visit.

Let's take a moment to talk about something we all find to be a wonder of nature: the northern lights. So, these lights are caused when electrically-charged particles that come directly from the sun manage to get into the Earth's atmosphere and collide with the particles there. Even though it is spoken about very often, it is rather difficult to catch one of these in nature without prior planning and consulting with the weather channel.

It is more of a 'right time, right place' sort of scenario. However, if you want a better shot of seeing the result of these little particles fighting it out, stop by the Northern Lights Space and Science Centre, which offers a simulated version of this spectacle.

This incoming section of the trip is a shorter five-hour drive of 272 miles to Whitehorse, a hub for cultural and outdoor activities. It is the largest city in northern Canada, so you can imagine just how many sights and wonderful places there are. You can stay busy at any of these following destinations, or feel free to improvise as you go along:

- The Yukon Wildlife Preserve - A safe space for animals such as the Canada lynx, the Rocky Mountain elk, the Alaska Yukon moose, woodland caribou, red foxes, arctic foxes, and more than 90 different species of birds. If you wish to see or even feed these lovely creatures in their natural habitats, all you need to do is park your RV in the designated spot, walk right into the log reception building, pay the fees, and head on over to a world of fantastic beasts. The rates go as such:

Age	Guided Bus Tour	Self-Guided Walking Tour
Adults (18 years and older)	$22.00	$15.00
Youth (13-17 year-old students with an ID card)	$10.00	$8.00
Children (4-12 years-old)	$7.00	$5.00
Toddlers (under 4 years of age)	Free Admission	Free Admission
Seniors (65 years and older)	$20.00	$12.00

*Important things to note: the park does not allow pets, nor does it have running water (you are strongly suggested to bring your own).

- Takhini Hot Springs - In business for over a century, these hot springs are one of the most relaxing destinations on the list. The hot springs are packed with rich minerals beneficial for your skin and overall health. You will have to bring your own shoes for the change rooms, and while you can rent a towel or a bathing suit, I recommend you just bring your own and save the pocket money on it. Regular admission rates go as follows, although prices are bound to change ever-so-slightly depending on the season:

Adults (18 years and older)	$12.50
Seniors (60 years and older)	$11.00
Youth (13-17 year-olds with an ID)	$10.00

Children (4-12 years)	$9.00
Family Pass (Valid for five family members, maximum)	$35.00

- Emerald Lake - Located in the Yoho National Park and typically quieter than Lake Louise, the Emerald Lake is very accordingly named for its light turquoise shimmering waters. There are astounding views of the lake, particularly when you spend the day walking or hiking around its perimeter. A helpful tip: arrive early for a viable parking space, and do give it ago at renting a canoe and floating in the tranquil surroundings. Remember to try to make a reservation at a nearby lodge if you intend to stay for a longer period of time.

S.S. Klondike National Historic Site - A fantastic location where not only you could explore the history of the Klondike Gold Rush days through saloons, the Klondike Goldfields, a guided tour from a historical figure, and so much more.

Other than beautiful outdoor settings, this site also has an interactive escape room involving solving a real-life murder that took place back in 1903. The prices vary depending on the season, as most parks do, but for the most part, we are looking at a rate of $6.30 per person for the general site, and $22.00 per person for the escape room activity.

The final portion of your trip takes you about 11 hours and 589 miles to Fairbanks, Alaska. This is the gateway to the interior of the U.S. state of Alaska. Let's look at a few outdoor and indoor activities bound to strike your fancy as well as the members of your RV group:

- The Arctic National Wildlife Refuge - With an array of almost 200 species of birds and four dozen mammal species, this refuge is one of the most amazing locations in the entire world. You can view moose, gray wolves, grizzly bears, Arctic foxes, caribou, river otters, polar bears, whales, oxen, woodpeckers, owls, hawks, or plenty of fish if you wish it. The refuge stands as a pristine location perfect for understanding the delicate balance between man and nature.

- The Museum of the North - If you feel like delving deeper into Alaskan natural and cultural history with the Gallery of Alaska (collected objects from five geographic regions), the Special Exhibits (more short-term exhibits based on specialized time periods), the Family Room (puzzles, games, kid-friendly environment), and the Rose Berry Alaska Art Gallery (with a compilation of 2,000 years' worth of Alaska Native objects, paintings, sculptures, and photographs). From September 1st to May 31st, the museum is open from Monday through Saturday, 9am-5pm. Summer hours go from June 1st to August 31st, open daily from 9am-7pm. The admission rates are listed as such:

Adults (Ages 15 and up)	$14.00
Youth (Ages 5-14)	$8.00
Museum Movie Ticket	$5.00

- Black Spruce Dog Sledding - Now, who does not love dog sledding? The best part is you do not even need snow in order to visit this location during the hotter seasons since the sled dogs are harnessed onto a five-passenger wheeled vehicle light enough for them to handle without any difficulties. If you are not too into sledding, you can also just go on the Husky Hiking Tour during late May to early September and walk along the Alaskan tundra accompanied by friendly, fluffy Husky puppies or adult dogs.

- Golden Heart Plaza - Whether you prefer Italian, Greek, Thai, seafood, or pure Alaskan cuisines, some of the best restaurants at Fairbanks are located in the Golden Heart Plaza. With an astounding clock tower, the plaza is used for several seasonal events; during the summer, it is bursting with colorful blooming flowers, and during the winter it is decorated with cheerful Christmas lights. Definitely more of a destination for someone interested in the town life. If you wish to go on a quiet, serene walk and just observe the parks and buildings of downtown Fairbanks accompanied by flowers, go to the Chena Riverwalk during the month of May.

- Ballaine Lake - Has a 1.2-mile trail for horseback riding, hiking, or biking, and is located near the University of Alaska. Admire trees, birds, the occasional raccoon and squirrel, flowers, and the glimmering lake itself as you go for a nice leg-stretching walk.

Another couple more places to check out consist of the Palace Theatre (excellent plays about frontier life), Hagelbarger Viewpoint (one of the highest lookouts in Fairbanks, and one of the most impressive scenic views), Fairbanks Children's Museum (interactive educational games, maps, and activities for children), Pioneer Air Museum (antique aircrafts on display), Wedgewood Wildlife Sanctuary (smaller than the Arctic National Wildlife Refuge, but still just as worthwhile),

Georgeson Botanical Garden (collection of flowers established back in 1991), Fountainhead Antique Auto Museum (beautiful antique vehicles), Fairbanks Ice Museum (large ice sculpture displays and exhibits), and Creamer's Field Migratory Waterfowl Refuge (old dairy farm turned into a waterfowl refuge).

Suggested RV Trip #2

Another trip option is to start in Valleyview, Alberta and travel 1,032 miles south along the Yellowhead Highway to Winnipeg. This trip takes almost 17 hours, but there is a lot to stop and see along the way. Let's take a look at this trip.

Begin in Valleyview. To the north, you can visit the Peace River for water and hiking activities. A short way to the west you can reach Dawson Creek and the Alaska Highway. With so much to see and do at this crossroads, you may want to spend a night or two while planning out the rest of your trip.

Suggested RV Park in Valleyview

In the town of Valleyview, you can stay at Sherks RV Park. It is open May 1st to September 30th with an average rate of $45. It is a pet-friendly park. There are 56 spaces with the following amenities:

- ☐ Internet
- ☐ Laundry
- ☐ RV Service
- ☐ RV Supplies
- ☐ Self-Service RV Wash
- ☐ Restrooms
- ☐ Showers
- ☐ Ice
- ☐ Horseshoes
- ☐ Archery Range
- ☐ Recreational Hall
- ☐ Playground

If you choose not to stay in Valleyview, it is a short drive of about an hour and a half or 106 miles to Whitecourt. Located along the banks of the Athabasca River, you can explore some of the most natural woodlands in Canada. 12 miles outside of town you'll find Carson Pegasus Provincial Park. For indoor fun, you can visit the Eagle River Casino for adults and Travel Plaza for families.

SUGGESTED RV PARK-1 IN WHITECOURT

In Whitecourt, you have the option to stay at Eagle River Tourism RV Park. It is open all year with an average rate of $35 to $40 per night. It is a pet-friendly park with restrictions on size and quantity. It has 107 sites with the following amenities:

- ☐ Internet
- ☐ Ice
- ☐ RV Service
- ☐ ATM Machines
- ☐ Snack Bar
- ☐ Restrooms
- ☐ Showers
- ☐ Groceries
- ☐ Laundry
- ☐ Restaurant
- ☐ Playground

SUGGESTED RV PARK-2 IN WHITECOURT

Another option in Whitecourt is the Whitecourt Lions Campground. It is open from April 15th to October 15th with an average rate of $32 to $39 per night. It is a pet-friendly park. There are 72 spaces with the following amenities:

- ☐ Internet
- ☐ Laundry
- ☐ RV Service
- ☐ Restrooms
- ☐ Showers
- ☐ Ice
- ☐ Playground

Our incoming RV route consists of 113 miles of about two hours to Edmonton. Here you connect to the historic Yellowhead Highway. Edmonton is the capital city of Alberta, so as you can imagine there are tons of activities to check out. Some of these include:

- The West Edmonton Mall - With the size of 48 city blocks, this is the largest shopping mall in North America, so be prepared for a long day of sightseeing. There are hundreds of stores, restaurants, a casino, mini-golf courses, a waterpark equipped with an immense wave pool and waterslides, an aquarium, and amusement park rides. In other words, the mall is an experience in itself.

- The Muttart Conservatory - This conservatory features biomes inside huge glass pyramids, with a fourth pyramid dedicated to demonstrating the changing of the seasons through its display of ornamental flowering plants. The other three pyramids consist of the Temperate pyramid, the Arid pyramid, and the Tropical pyramid. The conservatory also has a lovely café offering local, fresh ingredients. The standard hours go from 10am-5pm for the week, except on Wednesdays and Thursdays when it stretches to 9 pm. The rates are as such as of this current year, but check out the conservatory's website before visiting to confirm the prices have not changed:

Child (Aged 2-12)	$6.50
Youth (Aged 13-17)	$10.50
Adult (Aged 18-64)	$12.50

Senior (Aged 65 and up)	$10.50
Family (Maximum of Seven People)	$37.00

*Children under two years of age are free admissions.

- Edmonton Valley Zoo - Home to over 350 animals, including an absolutely adorable Asian elephant named Lucy, the Edmonton Valley Zoo is an excellent option for fans of the animal kingdom and the younger members of your RV group.

- TELUS World of Science - Featuring an IMAX movie theatre, the Zeidler dome, seasonal exhibits, the S.P.A.C.E. Gallery, the Science Garage, the Body Fantastic, a Myth Busters program, and the largest food and drink laboratory in Edmonton, this is a remarkable place to learn, and have fun as you are surrounded by some of the best scientific resources in Canada.

- Elk Island National Park - This national park has the right to boast about having the second largest population of elk, mule deer, moose, white-tailed deer, and bison. There is guided snowshoeing during the winter and early spring months as well as interpretive programs that teach you all about the indigenous populations in the area, as well as the animals you are about to see.

- Downtown Edmonton - Enjoy the occasional year-round festival at the plaza, the beautiful surrounding buildings, art galleries, antique shops, delicious restaurants, breweries, and snack bars. You can also relax for a long stroll, a quick swim, or a picnic at the Legislature Grounds.

- Hawrelak Park - A 68-hectare park packed with a lovely lake, as well as picturesque bike and jogging trails, plush grass hills, a skating and ice rinks, food concession places, playground areas for children, and fountains. It is a perfect location for various seasonal events and festivals, so keep an eye out and make sure you visit the website for more information on which events interest you the most.

- Snow Valley Ski Club - For those who are active and prefer something a bit more strenuous than hiking or walking, the Snow Valley Ski Club is a profit-free organization that is aimed mostly at beginner skiers and snowboarders, although there is a section for individuals who want more of a challenge at an advanced level. Heads-up: the club might be closed under extreme weather conditions, so make sure to check with their website ahead of time.

Suggested RV Park in Spring Lake

Just north of Edmonton, you can choose to stay in the small town of Spring Lake at the Spring Lake RV Resort. It is open May 1st to September 30th with an average rate of $50 to $61 per night. It is pet-friendly with restrictions on the breed. There are 200 sites with the following amenities:

☐ Internet

- ☐ Laundry
- ☐ Ice
- ☐ RV Supplies
- ☐ Groceries
- ☐ Restrooms
- ☐ Showers
- ☐ Playground
- ☐ Horseshoes
- ☐ Boat Dock

SUGGESTED RV PARK IN STONY PLAIN

In the outskirts of Edmonton, in the small town of Stony Plain, you can stay at the Camp'n Class RV Park. It is open all year with an average rate of $52 to $57 each night. It is pet-friendly with restrictions on breed and quantity with an additional fee. There are 77 sites with the following amenities:

- ☐ Internet
- ☐ Laundry
- ☐ Restrooms
- ☐ RV Service
- ☐ Shower
- ☐ RV Supplies

- ☐ Cable
- ☐ Ice
- ☐ Recreational Hall

SUGGESTED RV PARK-1 IN EDMONTON

Within Edmonton itself, you have two excellent options. First is the Diamond Grove RV Campground, which is open all year with an average rate of $47 to $52 per night. It is a pet-friendly park. There are 242 sites with the following amenities:

- ☐ Internet
- ☐ Laundry
- ☐ Ice
- ☐ Snack Bar
- ☐ Restrooms
- ☐ Showers
- ☐ RV Supplies
- ☐ Groceries
- ☐ Hot Tub
- ☐ Recreational Hall
- ☐ Playground

SUGGESTED RV PARK-2 IN EDMONTON

Also within Edmonton is the Glowing Embers, RV Park. It is pet-friendly and open all year with an average rate of $45 to $50. It is a pet-friendly park. It has 288 sites with the following amenities:

- ☐ Internet
- ☐ Laundry
- ☐ RV Service
- ☐ Restrooms
- ☐ RV Supplies
- ☐ Showers
- ☐ Metered Gas
- ☐ Self-Service RV Wash
- ☐ Ice
- ☐ Recreational Hall
- ☐ Exercise Room
- ☐ Game Room
- ☐ Playground

The next leg of your trip guides you 156 miles or about a two-and-a-half hour drive to Lloydminster. This town was founded in 1903 and today sits on the border between Alberta and Saskatchewan provinces. Learn about the area by visiting the Lloydminster Cultural and Science Center. In the summer, there are several seasonal events you can view, including a rodeo, an art festival, and a Colonial Days fair.

Next, you head to North Battleford in a short hour-long, 86-mile trip. This town is located along the North Saskatchewan River. View the agricultural heritage of the area at the Western Development Museum, or test your luck at the Gold Eagle Casino. Other sightseeing activities include the Table Mountain Regional Park ski facilities, the Chapel Gallery, and the Fred Light Museum (boasting a collection of more than 250 firearms).

Another short 86-mile trip of about an hour takes you to Saskatoon. This is the largest city in Saskatchewan and offers a range of outdoor and cultural activities. Start by hiking the Meewasin Trail that takes you along the river and through a number of historical sites and the opportunity to visit several museums along the way.

Some key locations include the Wanuskewin Heritage Park (featuring artwork and history of the Native American culture), Meewasin Northeast Swale (diverse ecosystems containing thousands of years of history for both the natural and the cultural aspects of the world), Nutrien Playland at Kinsmen Park (Ferris wheel, carousels, a park train, water areas, all in a huge open space, no admission fees), the Museum of Antiquities, and the Saskatchewan Railway Museum.

SUGGESTED RV PARK IN SASKATOON

If you need a place to stay for a night or two, then head to the Campland RV Resort. It is open April 4th to November 1st and costs an average of $42 to $46 per night. It is pet-friendly with restrictions on quantity.

There are 132 sites with the following amenities:

- ☐ Internet
- ☐ Laundry
- ☐ Ice
- ☐ Restrooms

- ☐ RV Supplies
- ☐ Groceries
- ☐ Showers
- ☐ Heated Pool
- ☐ Playground

When you are ready, get back on the road and drive 204 miles, or about 3 hours south to Yorkton. The main draw of this small town is fishing. The landscape here is full of lakes with plenty of opportunities for pike, trout, and walleye fishing. This area is also home to one of the top beaches in Canada at Good Spirit Lake Provincial Park.

The last portion of the trip is a 281-mile, five-hour drive south to Winnipeg. This is where the Yellowhead Highway ends. You will come face to face with a cultural center in Canada that features numerous museums and festivals. Let's check out a few activities and destinations here.

7 Must-See Places Around Winnipeg

Folklorama - Visiting in the late summer gives you a chance to see the largest and longest running festival in Canada, known as Folklorama. It features crafts, music, and dances from numerous cultures around the world.

Assiniboine Park Zoo - Polar bears! Almost 50 species of birds and mammals, 14 species of amphibians and reptiles, and 26 species of fish and invertebrates, this zoo stands as one of the most remarkable destinations in the area.

Leo Mol Sculpture Garden - A vast collection of exquisite bronze sculptures arranged amidst fields of flowers, ponds, fountains, bridges, and intricate gazebos. The park is one of the territories near the zoo, and also offers small art exhibits in the park, delightful restaurants, and a miniature steam train.

Fort Garry Hotel - An allegedly haunted historic landmark in Winnipeg, the hotel opened back in December 1913 and has since then turned into the Fort Garry Hotel, Spa and Conference Centre. Despite the rumors of the ghost in Room 202, one cannot deny this building is gorgeous inside and out and is well-worth a visit (and perhaps a stay in one of their 240 rooms).

The Forks - The meeting space of both the Red and Assiniboine rivers now turned into a hub for entertainment, art, food, and recreation. In the past, it used to be key in the fur trade of the 18th and 19th centuries, according to the Canadian Encyclopedia. In 1974, the Forks was named a National Historic Site of Canada. Here you can check out various stores, a nine-acre park, restaurants, live music, theatre plays, and so much more.

Exchange District BIZ - Downtown Winnipeg was founded in 1881 and was also deemed another National Historic Site of Canada. The downtown covers about 20 city blocks full of historic buildings, bustling small and large shops, family-owned and more commercial restaurants, as well as their own street fairs and seasonal festivals/events.

FortWhyte Alive - After seeing all of these places, you might want a wee break with some fresh air. What better place for some self-guided peace and quiet than 640 acres of nothing more than trees, trails, wildlife, and small mini-towns to explore?

SUGGESTED RV PARK IN PORTAGE LA PRAIRIE

North of Winnipeg in the small town of Portage La Prairie an excellent place to stay is Miller's Camping Resort. It is open May 1st to October 1st with an average rate of $33 to $45 per night. It is a pet-friendly park with restrictions on quantity. There are 192 sites with the following amenities:

- ☐ Internet
- ☐ Laundry
- ☐ RV Service
- ☐ Ice
- ☐ Restrooms
- ☐ Showers
- ☐ RV Supplies
- ☐ Snack Bar
- ☐ Groceries
- ☐ Heated Pool
- ☐ Playground
- ☐ Horseshoes
- ☐ Pedal Carts
- ☐ Game Room
- ☐ Bike Rentals

SUGGESTED RV PARK IN ST. FRANCIS XAVIER

Another option closer to Winnipeg in the small town of St. Francois Xavier is the Winnipeg West KOA. It is open April 15th to October 15th with an average rate of $35 to $49 per night. It is a pet-friendly park. It has 96 sites and the following amenities:

- ☐ Internet
- ☐ ATM Machines
- ☐ Ice
- ☐ RV Supplies
- ☐ Fishing Supplies
- ☐ Snack Bar
- ☐ Restrooms
- ☐ Showers
- ☐ Groceries
- ☐ Laundry
- ☐ Heated Pool
- ☐ Playground

SUGGESTED RV PARK IN WINNIPEG

Lastly, if you want to stay in Winnipeg, your best option is the Arrowhead RV Park. It is open April

15th to October 31st with an average rate of $37 to $47. It is a pet-friendly park. There are 54 spaces with the following amenities:
- ☐ Internet
- ☐ Restrooms
- ☐ Showers
- ☐ RV Service
- ☐ Laundry
- ☐ Horseshoes
- ☐ Recreational Hall
- ☐ Playground

RV Camping at National Parks in Alberta

No matter where you plan to travel in Alberta, be sure to set aside some time to drive through or visit at least one of these stunning National Parks. Alberta is home to four National Parks, some of which I have mentioned, and a few which were left out specifically for this section.

Banff National Park. Part of the Rocky Mountain range, this is the first national park in Canada, founded in 1885. Mountain peaks, lakes, and wildlife are abundant here as well.

Elk Island National Park. Responsible for saving the bison from near extinction. Nowadays, there is an active conservation program at this park, and you will get an excellent chance to see this majestic animal, along with many other hoofed creatures.

Jasper National Park. Features a vast array of natural sights from glaciers and canyons to lakes and waterfalls. There is no shortage of outdoor activities, including hiking, swimming, skiing, and fishing. There are even a few soothing hot springs to enjoy and relax in.

Waterton Lakes National Park. Located where the Rocky Mountains meet the Alberta prairies. It is a magical experience to visit this location while all the flowers are in full bloom.

BRITISH COLUMBIA

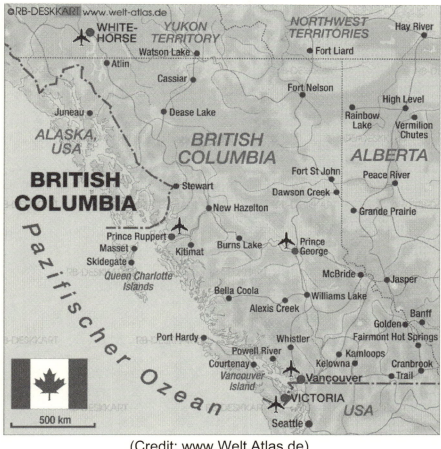

(Credit: www.Welt.Atlas.de)

The western province in Canada, and the only province where you can travel from mountain to desert in an alarmingly short period of time. In between, you can enjoy bodies of water such as lakes, marshes, rivers, and streams. These ecosystems are home to an abundance of wildlife living at various national parks.

There are five main climates in British Columbia, as we will cover in this introduction. Winters along the coastal area are temperate, and snow doesn't stay on the ground for too long before melting away. During the spring and fall, the weather can be warm and pleasant, so it is recommended to bring a light sweater for the colder temperatures during nightfall, or in case of cool breezes.

Ideal times to visit are June and September, as the weather is just perfect. In the core of the province, you can experience hot summers with temperatures easily climbing into the low-80 degrees Fahrenheit. That means you will need a hat, shorts, and plenty of sunblock or coconut oil.

Unless you are taking the RV trip that guides you from Alberta through British Columbia and into Alaska, there is one specific RV trip that is worth your time only in British Columbia. It is a relatively short drive, so you may be able to combine it with your itinerary on your way back from Alberta.

SUGGESTED **RV T**RIP

An excellent RV adventure trip starts in the capital of Vancouver and takes you across Highway 99 north, before circling back down south through Fraser Canyon. There are plenty of outdoor activities and a lot of rugged hiking for the adventurous traveler. However, there is also plenty of history to be seen along the way as well for the less outdoors-oriented traveler. In total, the trip takes 370 miles and is only about an eight-hour drive. Let's take a look at this route in detail.

Start your trip in Vancouver and the surrounding areas. Spend several days taking advantage of all the activities here if you wish to, or just get right on the road with the intention of spending time in the big city once you return at the end of the route. For a unique experience, take the Capilano Suspension Bridge where you can explore the coastal rainforest from the treetops. For the indoor shopper, Vancouver is home to the largest mall in British Columbia, so that is bound to be the highlight of the trip for any mindful shopper in the RV.

Be sure to visit the Dr. Sun-Yat Sen Classical Garden too, which was named one of the top city gardens by National Geographic. As a cosmopolitan city, there are several activities both in the priced and free categories, from museums, historic parks, zoos, restaurants, nightclubs, malls, natural reserves, and open markets.

I highly recommend browsing the internet for the categories you are most interested in seeing and planning your itineraries from there. Another excellent way to get to know Vancouver is simply to explore it without having a particular place in mind, on the other hand.

Suggested RV Park in Burnaby

Whether you are at the start or the end of your trip, there are two great places to stay in the small towns surrounding Vancouver. In the town of Burnaby, there is the Burnaby Cariboo RV Park. It is open all year with an average rate of $62 to $71 per night. It is a pet-friendly park. There are 212 sites with the following amenities:

- ☐ Internet
- ☐ ATM Machines
- ☐ Cable
- ☐ RV Supplies
- ☐ Restrooms
- ☐ Showers
- ☐ Ice
- ☐ Laundry
- ☐ Groceries
- ☐ Self-Service RV Wash
- ☐ Heated Pool
- ☐ Hot Tub
- ☐ Horseshoes
- ☐ Game Room
- ☐ Exercise Room
- ☐ Recreational Hall
- ☐ Playground

SUGGESTED RV PARK IN SURREY

Another option is the small town of Surrey. Here you can stay at Hazelmere RV Park. It is open all year with an average rate of $44 to $48 per night. It is a pet-friendly park. It features 198 sites with the following amenities:

- ☐ Internet
- ☐ Laundry
- ☐ Ice
- ☐ RV Supplies
- ☐ Groceries
- ☐ Restrooms
- ☐ Showers
- ☐ Cable
- ☐ Heated Pool
- ☐ Hot Tub
- ☐ Horseshoes
- ☐ Pedal Carts
- ☐ Recreational Hall
- ☐ Mini Golf
- ☐ Playground
- ☐ Exercise Room

When you're ready to start your trip, drive 82 miles to Whistler, which is approximately a two-hour long drive. This resort town is located at the base of some of the top ski mountain destinations in the world, such as Whistler Blackcomb, Whistler Mountain, and Blackcomb Peak.

It is also home to numerous summer activities at the Brandywine Falls Provincial Park (with its 229-foot waterfall and volcanic formations), the Green Lake (the largest lake in Whistler), the Rainbow Park (includes a dog park for your furry companion), Superfly Ziplines, and the Shannon Falls Provincial Park (with British Columbia's third largest waterfall). Year-round, people take delight in going for a few gondola rides or perhaps for a walk on the Peak Suspension Bridge.

Once you are finished exploring this destination and its natural wonders, you can drive another 81 miles or about two hours to the town of Lillooet. This town got its start during the Gold Rush, and today is a popular destination for fishing and swimming. For history buffs, it is recommended to visit the Old Suspension Bridge and the Lillooet Museum. Some other activities include going to Fort Berens Estate Winery for a bit of wine tasting or hiking in Cayoosh Creek.

The next stop is a quick one-hour drive consisting of 54 miles down the road to Cache Creek, located at the junction of two major roadways and a popular destination for tourists. If you want to spend your day in the great outdoors, head over to Juniper Beach Provincial Park, for those traveling with children, you should make a trip to the McAbee Fossil Beds, where you can explore over 80 petrified plant species.

After 120 miles and just over two hours, you will reach the town of Hope, which is surrounded by mountains on three sides and is located at the heart of where main rivers meet. Established back in 1848, its position offered convenient access to the trading business during the Gold Rush.

The town features unique art displays and is known for chainsaw competitions. There is no shortage of outdoor adventures here, what with the old railway Othello Tunnels, the historic Fort Hope, the Silver Lake, and the Nicolum River Provincial Park, to name a few.

The last portion of your trip consists of 33 miles to Chilliwack. Most people traveled through this area on their way for potential fortune during the Gold Rush in 1857. Today, the town hosts a popular art and music scene. For outdoor adventures, head to Cultus Lake and the surrounding mountain peaks and trails. For bird-watching, head to the Great Blue Heron Nature Reserve. Some more activities and destinations include:

The Chilliwack Tulip Festival - There are those who like flowers and gardening, then there are those who would see 10,000 tulips in full bloom as an once-in-a-lifetime, extremely appreciated experience. The Tulip Festival has been active for a little over a decade, making it the largest and oldest tulip festival in western Canada, according to their very informative website, tulipsofthevalley.com.

Dickens Sweets & British Museum - Named after well-renowned British writer Charles Dickens, this shop is a dream come true for those with a deep love for tea, all things sweet, and all things British. Their famous tea room has over 175 different flavors of loose tea leaves, while Pickwick's Bakery offers traditional scones, savory pies, pasties and turnovers, rolls, dessert bars and squares, and cakes. They also offer cake decorating lessons, in case you are interested in learning something new about baking during your RV experience.

Chilliwack Community Forest - Packed with plenty of hiking and biking trails, this quaint park does tend to get busy during rush hours, so an early arrival works best as long as you make the most of your morning, and leave for lunch in the afternoon.

Chilliwack Cultural Centre - Located in downtown Chilliwack, this performing arts venue offers various plays, exhibits, festivals, and both local and international events and performances. Visit their website and see what events are in store for your planned dates.

Bridal Falls Provincial Park - If the Community Forest sounds like it is too small for your adventurous soul, you can always raise it up a notch by going to the Bridal Veil Falls Provincial Park. Whether it is for a picnic, walk, jog, or hike, this is a worthwhile place if you love being surrounded by tall red cedar and maple trees, songbirds, and deer on your way to the mystical 122-meter waterfall.

Once you are satisfied with your exploration of the surrounding areas, you can circle back to Vancouver to end your trip or head off to other parts of British Columbia you would like to revisit.

RV Camping at National Parks in British Columbia

If you have time, bask in the natural beauty of British Columbia from one of the many national parks in the area.

Glacier National Park. In the winter you can ski through deep snow, and in the summer you can hike through serene, sweet-scented cedar forests. History buffs can visit the site of Canada's transcontinental railway completion at Rogers Pass and learn more about the work and effort behind each one of those metal tracks.

Gulf Islands National Park Reserve. These islands are scattered throughout the Salish Sea and are a great place to see rare animal species (seal pups, orcas, porpoises, black-tailed deer, purple martins, sea lions) and unique ecosystems (tide pools, for instance). It is a great place to enjoy nature by boat or on land. Pets are allowed so long as they are kept on a leash at all times, and remember never to litter and never feed or disrupt the wildlife in any way, shape, or form.

Gwaii Haanas National Park Reserve, National Marine Conservation Area Reserve and Haida Heritage Site. The islands here are full of lush rainforest and hot pools while the seas are brimming with wildlife in the underwater kelp forests, the shallows, and tide pools. A few of the creatures you will see are dolphins, sea lions, puffins, neon anemones, whales, sea stars, crabs, seals, orcas, and plenty of varieties of birds. This is also a culturally-historic location with carved poles and longhouses of the Haida people who co-manage the territory.

Kootenay National Park. This park features diverse terrain ranging from icy, stoic glaciers to widespread grasslands. Located along the historic Banff-Windermere Highway, this is an excellent spot for a scenic drive.

Mount Revelstoke National Park. Here you can enjoy beautiful, sprawling wildflower meadows. This park is great for a leisure day of driving and enjoying the outdoors while stopping every now and then for a quick stretching session, a picnic, or simply to take in your surroundings.

Pacific Rim National Park Reserve. This is a unique park on the west coast of Canada, where you can surf, learn about the Nuu-chah-nulth culture, hike along the coastline, or paddle away in a canoe or kayak. Featuring rainforests on land and kelp forests in the ocean, the wildlife-viewing opportunities you get here are priceless.

Yoho National Park. Remember how we mentioned the Emerald Lake a few sections back? Yoho National Park has this particular turquoise-colored body of water, as well as Takakkaw Falls, Lake O'Hara, and Wapta Falls. The park, in general, is located along the Great Divide, making it a fantastic place to experience the beauty of majestic snow-coated mountains up close.

MANITOBA

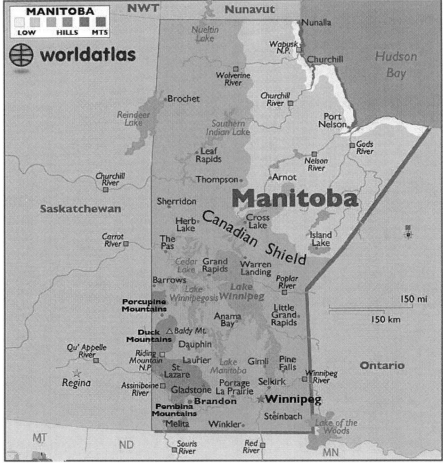

(Credit: World Atlas)

Of the three Prairie Provinces in Canada, Manitoba is the farthest east. It is a fairly level province with most of the southern part being agricultural land, and the northern part mostly tundra and permafrost. Nearly two-thirds of the 500 bird species that call

Canada home are found in this province due to the high number of lakes, rivers, and marshes where they can rest and nest in.

It is also an excellent place to go to view other kinds of wildlife since it has the highest density of moose, elk, and black bears in the country. You might want to be especially careful with never littering, staying on the marked paths and trails as to not find yourself in the territory of any potentially disgruntled large mammals and birds, and generally equipping yourself with plenty of water.

The climate in Manitoba is warm and sunny in the summer, along with freezing and bright winters. During July and August, the afternoon temperatures are an average of 80 to 90 degrees Fahrenheit. In the winter, most daytime temperatures average well below freezing, so remember to be dressed for the occasion in warm clothing and hiking boots with thick wool socks.

Over half of the annual precipitation happens in the summer months (you know it, raincoat and rain boots time). The heaviest snowfall occurs in the northeast at the Duck and Riding Mountains.

Due to the smaller size of this province, most planned RV routes are going to include other provinces. The Yellowhead Highway is a popular travel option that takes people into Manitoba or, if you do it in reverse, can start in Manitoba. See the Alberta listing above for this route. Otherwise, there is one city that you must visit during your stay in the Manitoba vicinity.

SUGGESTED CITY VISIT

Brandon is conveniently located along the Trans-Canada highway. At first, it looks like a prairie town, but when you look deeper, it has a lot of things to see and do. It is actually the second largest city in Manitoba, with a diverse range of historic buildings, museums, restaurants, shops, and parks, so you are sure to find something to keep you busy either outdoors or indoors.

If you are interested in history, you must take a walk through the downtown area, which is home to a national historic site and other 12 provincial historic sites. Most of these sites function as current cafes, restaurants, and boutiques. So, while strolling around to view historic buildings, you'll also be able to sample local flavors and cuisines. You can also join a residential walking tour to see all the architectural styles in the area with a guide knowledgeable on the subject.

Another great place is the Daly House Museum, home of the first mayor of Brandon. Here you can see a recreated general store and a Victorian garden that allows you to get a better idea of what life back in the 19th century was like. You can also learn more about the area at the Riverbank Discovery Centre.

No historical tour is complete without a visit to the Royal Canadian Artillery Museum. This museum is located at the Canadian Forces Base Shilo and features a wide array of heavy weapons on display. There are also numerous historical military artifacts in five indoor galleries. Nearby, there is also the Commonwealth Air Training Plane Museum. Located in an original hanger, this museum discusses the history of 50,000 pilots training at 14 air bases in Manitoba in WWII.

Brandon is a town of festivals and no matter what time of year you visit there is always some type of festival happening. There are three livestock and agricultural fairs held during the year. In the summer, there is the Folk, Music and Art Festival. In the winter, there is the Brandon Winter Festival that features cultures, food, music, and entertainment from around the world.

If you prefer to head outdoors for your adventure, then there are plenty of options as well. A short drive 60 miles north takes you to Riding Mountain National Park, where you can hike forests, marshes, and wetlands while catching a glimpse of various wildlife species. At the south gate for the park at Wasagaming you can take a Canadian safari.

Other options are the provincial parks of Rivers, Spruce Wood, Turtle Mountain, and William Lake. At these parks, you can take part in fishing, bird-watching, hiking, snowshoeing, cross-country skiing, and canoeing depending on the time of the year.

RV Camping at National Parks in Manitoba

The Manitoba province is home to two recommended National Parks.

Riding Mountain National Park. This park offers a range of outdoor possibilities, such as biking, jogging, or hiking trails and loops, camping, fishing, swimming, collecting edible berries (with the help of a guide as to prevent any poisoning incidents) watching the northern lights, or observe elk, wolves, bears, and bison. It is located where the forest meets the prairie, so a visit during any season would be perfect.

Wapusk National Park. This subarctic wilderness protects a large polar bear maternity den and is also home to over 200 bird species, caribou, wolverine, arctic hare, and foxes.

NEW BRUNSWICK

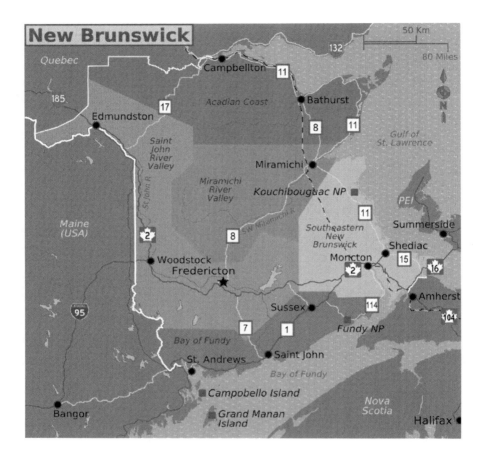

New Brunswick is a province known for its tides; they are the highest in the world, rising and falling the height of a four-story building. Discover this natural wonder and many other things when you visit this province.

New Brunswick is the largest of the three Maritime Provinces in Canada. It is located under Quebec and besides the state of Maine. The eastern boundary features sandy beaches and warm salt water only seen in Virginia. It is the only bilingual province in Canada with 33% of the population speaking French.

The northern half of New Brunswick has a continental climate of cold winters and warm summers. The southern half of the province is a more moderate maritime climate with mild winters and cooler summers. The warmest month is July with temperatures averaging in the 70 degrees Fahrenheit. Along the shore, the January average is 20 degrees Fahrenheit. Rain is evenly distributed throughout the year and fog is common in spring and early summer along the coastal area.

SUGGESTED RV TRIP

The best trip in New Brunswick is a short drive but has plenty of outdoor activities, so along the way be sure to stay a few nights at the National Park in the middle of your trip to enjoy everything the area has to offer. Let's take a look at this trip.

It is a short 107 miles and takes just over two hours of driving. It gets its start in Moncton. The town is beautiful in many ways and is also home to some unique attractions. The most visited spot is the gravity-defying Magnetic Hill. For whatever reason, this stretch of road seems to pull cars uphill. The surrounding area is also home to rivers, lakes, and coastlines offering some of the best fishing spots in the world.

Drive an hour down the road for 53 miles to Fundy National Park. Stop in here for a few days and explore as much as you wish for a wonderful outdoors experience. The Bay of Fundy is home to the highest tides in the world. Over a span of six hours you can watch the tides rise some 50 feet, so be very careful if you are on foot near the water. You can also visit the Hopewell Rocks, where you can view the "flowerpot rocks" at low tide and see them disappear as tides rise.

The Fundy Trail also offers options for biking, rappelling, and whale-watching.

Finally, drive 54 miles or about an hour down the road to St. Martins. The harbor and sea caves change twice a day along with the tides. You can visit the scenic Quaco Head Lighthouse, surrounded by salt marshes, tide pools, underwater kelp forests, and plenty of unique ecosystems.

RV Camping at National Parks in New Brunswick

Fundy National Park. Located in the middle of your drive, this is a great place to spend your time. You can watch the high tides, kayak the bay, or explore the seafloor during low tides and find all types of sea creatures and shells. You can also hike or bike through ancient forests. This is one of the best-known national parks in Canada.

Kouchibouguac National Park. This coastal park offers a lot of unique outdoor experiences. Sand dunes and estuaries give you excellent opportunities to view wildlife and local plants and flowers. There are also examples of Mi'kmaq and Acadian cultures. In the winter, there are plenty of snow activities such as sledding, snowshoeing, or skiing.

NEWFOUNDLAND AND LABRADOR

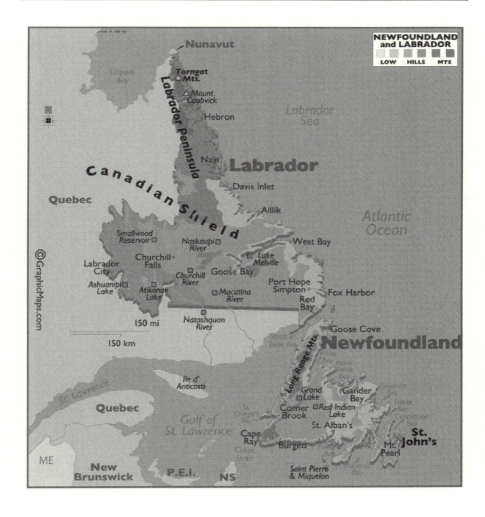

Newfoundland and Labrador is a province in Canada where an RV drive takes you to icebergs, whale-watching, and quaint coastal villages. There are two geographical parts to this province: the eastern part attached to the Canadian mainland and the island part located within the Gulf of St. Lawrence.

This is the far eastern province of Canada with a very small population spread across a large land mass. Most towns are located near the ocean and are mostly fishing villages along the rugged coastline. So, the food is absolutely great if you are a fan of crabs, fish, clams, and other seafood.

Newfoundland has the most maritime climate of the Atlantic Provinces, and this is clearly seen in spring and summer when it is cooler than most other provinces. The Labrador Current is cold from the glaciers and keeps July temperatures around 60 degrees Fahrenheit.

Inland, the temperature in the summer can go higher, but not by much. In Newfoundland, the sunny summer days are beautiful while the high temperatures in the afternoon can reach an average of 70 degrees Fahrenheit.

SUGGESTED RV TRIP

There isn't much in the way of lodging in this province, so staying in your RV at a national park is the best way to enjoy the beautiful scenery. The best RV trip is a short drive but gives you plenty to observe and do in the grand wilderness. It is a loop that guides you 197 miles in a little over four hours but allows you to catch all there is in this eastern province of Canada.

Start your trip at St. John's, the 500-year-old capital of the province. It is located among the steep hills of a sheltered harbor. This town has modern luxury mixed with the charm of a quaint, picturesque coastal village to offer you a unique travel destination. Here you can bask in stunning views of the Atlantic Ocean.

A short drive of 74 miles or about an hour and a half takes you to St. Mary's, a great place to watch birds or get out and explore the Cape St. Mary's Ecological Reserve. It is one of just seven seabird ecological reserves in the world.

When you are ready, you can drive about three hours or 123 miles to complete the loop back to St. John's.

RV Camping at National Parks in Newfoundland & Labrador

Akami-Uapishk-KakKasuak-Mealy Mountains National Park Reserve. Located in Labrador, this national park features the Mealy Mountains which are surrounded by glaciers with bare rock summits that overlook Lake Melville. A perfect place for a wilderness adventure.

Gros Morne National Park. From prairies and forests to the dry Tablelands and the glacier-carved fjords, this park has stunning shorelines and a diverse landscape; the geological oddities found here have earned the park a UNESCO World Heritage status. It is a great place to relax in the coastal community of Newfoundland, and to learn more about their cultural heritage through festivals, art exhibits, and galleries, as well as musical events.

Terra Nova National Park. Located along the dramatic Atlantic coastline, here you can walk along one of the long headlands and fjords to view whales or icebergs floating in the ocean. Inland, you can enjoy marshlands and wildlife-filled forests.

Torngat Mountains National Park. These mountains are home to polar bears and caribou. The land is still home to native Inuit. Visiting here allows you to view both nature and culture with a stunning backdrop.

NORTHWEST TERRITORIES

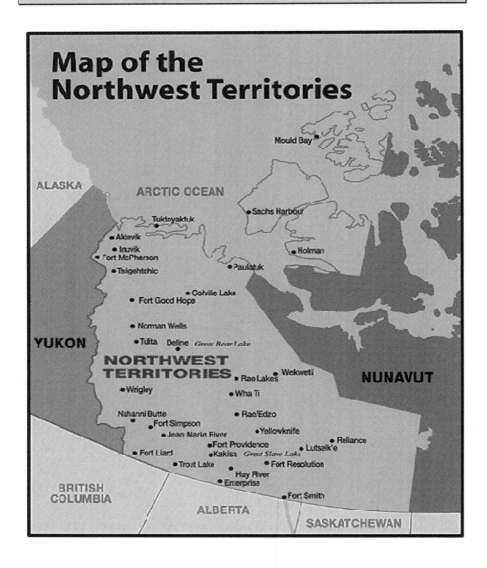

The Northwest Territories is a place with the endless sky and northern lights where you can record rare and unique wildlife such as the muskoxen, bison, and numerous birds. The best way to get around this rugged landscape is by RV, definitely.

The Northwest Territories is located north of British Columbia and Alberta. Despite this northern climate, the days here are often sunny and warm in the summer. In June, July, and August the temperatures can reach close to 90 degrees Fahrenheit and daylight can often be up to 24 hours. During the winter, temperatures can average fourteen to negative 40 degrees Fahrenheit.

SUGGESTED RV TRIP

The Northwest Territories is one of the least populated provinces in Canada and has plenty of wilderness for outdoor adventurers. The RV trip here is short but offers plenty of pit-stops to satiate your need for wilderness, trees, lakes, and fresh air. It is 249 miles and is about four and a half hours of driving time.

Start your trip in Fort Smith with a visit to the Northern Life Museum and Cultural Center to learn about the geology, wildlife, and plant life of the area as well as the First Nation heritage. Be sure to drive through or stay a few nights at the Wood Buffalo National Park, one of the largest buffalo and bison reserves in Canada. There are protected herds of bison that roam free, without any danger.

The next stop is about a three-hour drive or 169 miles to Hay River. This town is on the shore of the Great Slave Lake. It is the tenth largest lake in the world and the deepest one in North America, at over 2,000 feet into the deepest point.

You should head on over to the Mackenzie River, as it is home to the town of Fort Providence. This town offers a wide range of First Nations arts and crafts, as well as good launching points for water activities. To the north of town there is the Mackenzie Bison Sanctuary where the wood buffalo is protected, so you'll often see them standing near the road.

Another great destination is the town of Yellowknife that sits on the north shore of the lake. Being the capital city of the Northwest Territories, Yellowknife is distinctive for the Prince of Wales Northern

Heritage Center, dog sledding, the Snowking Winter Festival, and plenty of viewpoints at lakes and hilltops to gaze upon the night sky with the chance of seeing the Northern lights.

Once you are ready to leave Hay River, drive about an hour and a half or 80 miles down the road to Lady Evelyn Falls. This beautiful waterway is home to several waterfalls that are only honestly rivaled by Niagara Falls. There are several hiking trails for a proper walkthrough of your memorable surroundings.

RV Camping at National Parks in Northwest Territories

Aulavik National Park. One of the most remote national parks in Canada, consisting of more than 4,633 square miles of arctic territories in Banks Island. Its hills, badlands, valleys, seacoasts, and polar deserts are what make it a flexible opportunity to see untouched lands at their utmost peak of natural beauty.

Nahanni National Park Reserve. A World Heritage Site consisting of 11,583 square miles of land, it is overridden with plateaus, rivers, lakes, waterfalls, and mountain peaks. You may go on a paddling trip down the river, or perhaps for an aerial adventure on a biplane, or maybe testing your strength at a hiking trip in the alpines (not recommended for those who do not have prior training).

Naats'ihch'oh National Park Reserve. You can go canoeing in rough and wild waters, hiking rugged mountains and peaks, swimming in calm lakes, or quietly observing the birds, bears, sheep, mountain goats, and Cariou that stop by for a moment's rest. Note: This Park is recommended only for experienced adventurers unless you are accompanied by either a guide or someone who has previous training on the land.

Tuktut Nogait National Park. Made up of three major winding rivers and deep-set canyons, the park is home to rare caribou, muskoxen, wolves, and grizzly bears, to name a few. The park is open year-round, with visitor services available from 9am-4:30pm.

NOVA SCOTIA

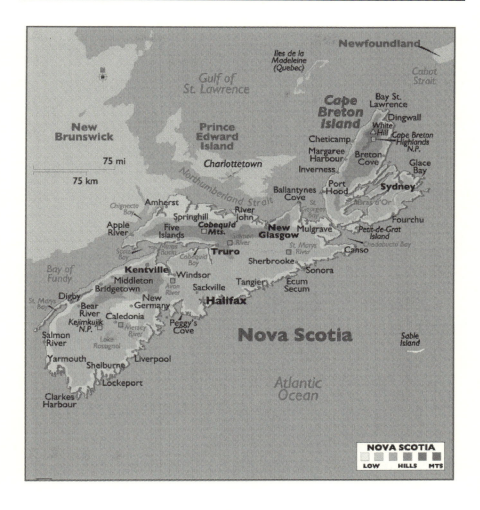

Nova Scotia is a peninsula on the southeastern coast of Canada which is connected to the province of New Brunswick and the North American mainland by the isthmus of Chignecto. The province is surrounded by numerous bays and estuaries, and most towns are located very close to the sea.

The climate in Nova Scotia is temperate, where summer temperatures in the daytime can average 70 degrees Fahrenheit with evening lows averaging 50 degrees Fahrenheit. If you are near the coast, then a sweater is best since there are cool breezes. Inland, the weather can be a little warmer by about ten degrees. In the spring and autumn, the temperature is often about ten degrees cooler.

SUGGESTED RV TRIP

Taking an RV trip in Nova Scotia takes you from a modern city to a quaint seaside village in 90 miles. The drive is a little over two hours, but there is plenty to see and do so you'll want to find a place to stay for a few nights to enjoy everything around you.

Start your trip out in the heart of Nova Scotia, Halifax. This waterfront city is the commercial and financial hub of the province. Equipped with its own casino, immense farmers' market, beautiful lakes, and lovely coastline villages, Halifax is a piece of paradise in itself. A few of the destinations you should definitely consider seeing here are:

- Halifax Seaport Farmers' Market - Leather creations, intricate jewelry, paintings, soaps and candles, photograph prints, warm golden bread, sweet cakes and candy, locally-grown crops, cream and milk, and only the freshest type of fish. This is the place where artisans, farmers, artists, bakers, and woodcarvers gather together to sell their magnificent creations and goods to the public. It is an amazing opportunity to know more about the product and the people around you.

- The Halifax Public Gardens - Founded in 1836, these Victorian gardens the oldest ones in North America. Throughout the year you can expect this place to host the summer concert series, walking tours, flower exhibits arranged by floral artists, as well as many more activities fit for all ages.

- Fisherman's Cove - This is a restored 200-year-old fishing village worthy of any type of individual. Unique crafts, food, drinks, oddities as well as deep-sea fishing and island tours are waiting for you.

- Maritime Museum of the Atlantic - The largest and oldest maritime museum in Canada, brimming with rich history about Nova Scotia's cultural heritage as a settlement so close to the ocean waves. You are welcome to learn all about the Titanic and Halifax's involvement in it's the tragic aftermath, the Halifax Explosion, the evolution of ships throughout the years, as well as seasonal exhibits.

- Peggy's Point Lighthouse - Even though Nova Scotia is known for having more than 160 historic lighthouses, this is part of the most well-known ones. Now, this is not the place for swimming, since there can be unexpectedly rough waves or currents beneath the surface that could be dangerous. So, the main tip is to stay on the dry, white-colored rocks.

- Downtown Halifax - International cuisines, pubs, and beer gardens, as well as furniture, clothing, and antique shops are waiting for you in downtown Halifax. With its older architecture, this is one of the best places for a more urban experience with excellent food, amazing surroundings, and great people.

- Crystal Crescent Beach Provincial Park - If you are more in the mood for bird-watching or hiking, the Crystal Crescent Beach Provincial Park offers you three beaches to choose from for your outdoors exploration.

- The Bluff Wilderness Hiking Trail - Up to speed for advanced hikers, there are four loops that take about three to four hours to complete (each) and covers various types of landscapes. You may expect evergreen forests, open granite barrens with glacial outcropping, over 100 types of lichens, and various lakes. Because there are no facilities available, you will have to bring plenty of water, food, a map, and a compass, and you are allowed to take your pups with you so long as they are on a leash at all times.

- Clam Harbour Beach Provincial Park - A natural beach where you may go on hikes, boardwalk strolls, a swim, or on a sandcastle-building competition. This location is especially kid-friendly since it features a shallow tidal stream of warm water on one side of the beach, so children can be warm as they float in a safe loop.

- Casino Nova Scotia - If you happen to have a lucky streak in Texas hold'em or blackjack, give any casino here a try. If you would rather be a spectator, there are also bunches of restaurants, slot machines, shopping malls, and plenty of space to walk on inside the establishment.

Whether you stay in this area and drive to the next point or decide to head on down the road, make sure you stop at Peggy's Cove. It is a short 28 miles and less than an hour drive from Halifax. Located along the south shore of Nova Scotia, there are plenty of landmarks to see here. At the entrance to St. Margaret's Bay you'll find the town's lighthouse that was built in 1915.

End your trip with about an hour drive for the 63 miles to Lunenburg. This town is a time capsule to the days of British colonial rule. The Old Town portion of this town holds UNESCO status, and once you visit, it will not be difficult to see why.

Some attractions include the Ovens Natural Park (learn more about the legends behind the Indian Cave, Captain Kidd, and the Cunard Family in their vintage campground by the shore), exploring the docked ships at the Lunenburg Harbour, tasting the unique and locally-produced liquor from Ironworks Distillery, visiting St. John's Anglican Church to admire the thought that went behind its creation, as well as the Fisheries Museum of the Atlantic for a lesson on the fishing trade and to see their aquarium.

RV Camping at National Parks in Nova Scotia

Cape Breton Highlands National Park. The world-famous Cabot Trail passes through this national park. There are 26 diverse hiking trails that take you through ocean vistas and deep canyons.

Kejimkujik National Park and Historic Site. This park has over 4,000 years of Mi'kmaq heritage. Visit to hike the forest or watch the harbor seals. There is plenty to see and discover at this national park.

Sable Island National Park Reserve. This remote national park is located on an island and offers plenty of opportunities to view noble wild horses, dive seemingly haunted and magnificent shipwrecks, and spot rare colorful birds of all feathers.

ONTARIO

The second largest province in Canada, Ontario is also the most populated and features a wide range of climates depending on where you go. Summers are often pleasant, with an average temperature in July of 70 degrees Fahrenheit in the southwest, to 60

degrees Fahrenheit in the eastern area. The northern portions are subarctic with July temperatures averaging 60 degrees Fahrenheit in the summer and negative 13 degrees Fahrenheit in January.

SUGGESTED RV TRIP

Despite its large size, you can see all or most of Ontario on a packed road trip of just 104 miles and about two hours. Make sure you make plenty of pit stops in key destinations. If you wish to spend a longer amount of time here, feel more than free to do so at your own pace and schedule by gathering inspiration from this incoming itinerary.

Start your trip out in the largest and most diverse city in Canada. Here you'll find no shortage of cultural, historical, and culinary experiences. Visit the CN Tower where you can enjoy breathtaking views of Lake Ontario while eating lunch in a revolving restaurant towering about 1,812 feet above the ground. Another way to see the area is with a 20-minute ferry to the Toronto Islands. Some more destinations to drop by include:

- **Algonquin Provincial Park** - If you are a fan of trout, this is the perfect place to fish, especially if you visit during May. This park is also equipped with eight campgrounds, 14 trails, thousands of lakes, and moose-viewing and bird-watching opportunities.

- **St. Lawrence Market** - Ranked the best food market in the world by National Geographic, the St. Lawrence Market is almost like one of the magical, extensive markets straight from a fantasy book. Originating back in the early 1800s, this destination consists of three buildings and hundreds of vendors selling locally grown fruits, seafood, and vegetables as well as handmade cheeses, sausages, baked goods, jams, wines, salted meats, sandwiches, caramels, and creams.

- **Butterfly Conservatory** - A glass-enclosed building containing over 2,000 rainforest butterflies that would be more than willing to rest on your shoulder, head, arms, or fingers if you are patient enough. The admission prices may vary, but as of the year this guide was written, they stand at the following:

Adults (Ages 13 and up)	$16.00
Children (Ages 6-12)	$10.25

- **Kensington Market** - It may not be as large at the St. Lawrence Market, but it does have more interesting stock to choose and pick from, all surrounded by live music from local and international musicians. It is the hub for a wide array of communities, with independent businesses, coffee shops, and a focus on the arts, it is definitely worth a visit.

- **Royal Ontario Museum** - Located in an impressive building, their exhibits and over 30 galleries vary depending on the season, but one thing is for certain: they are as educational as they are entertaining. The Museum is open every day from 10am to 5:30pm, except for December 25. Ticket rates are prone to vary, but the current prices are:

Adults (Ages 14 and Up)	$20.00
Children (Ages 4-14)	$14.00
Seniors (Ages 65+)	$17.00
Students (With A Valid Student ID)	$16.50
Youth (Ages 15-19)	$16.50
Infants (Ages 0-3)	Free Admission

- **Journey Behind the Falls** - How would you feel about coming face to face with lengthy 130-year-old tunnels with the rumble of a giant waterfall above you? If the thought thrills you instead of giving you minor claustrophobia, consider going on this adventure. Remember to bring a waterproof phone case, as well as everything you might need for a destination where you will definitely not stay dry as you descend 125 feet into the Horseshoe Falls.

- **Bruce Peninsula National Park** - The terms 'rugged beauty' have rarely had as much meaning as when it comes to this national park. Packed with giant rock formations at the foot of various mountains, cliff edges, towering cedar trees, orchids and wildflowers that put the colors of the rainbow to shame, and crystalline waters, this is an excellent location for wilderness fans everywhere.

- **Sandbanks Provincial Park** - Equipped with the world's largest baymouth barrier dune formation, three beaches, a wide array of birds, upkept trails crossing through the wetlands and dunes, the park is a perfect bucket list item for families and individuals alike.

- **Rideau Canal** - Approximately 125.6 miles in length, this UNESCO World Heritage Site waterway is a pretty fantastic way of seeing most of Toronto on skates (both roller skates and ice skates), on foot, on a boat, or on a bike.

- **Canada's Wonderland** - Get your daily dose of adrenaline by going on a ride at any of the roller coasters, splash works, slides, or thrill rides in Canada's Wonderland. If you are accompanied by children, there are the kids' rides and wading pools, as well as the fair food to consider. This park is also host to a series of special events during the holidays, so check their calendar to stay up to date on these.

- **Hockey Hall of Fame** - Home of the Stanley Cup, we have a perfect destination for fans of ice hockey. This museum is absolutely packed with historical facts, the largest collection of hockey artifacts from celebrated players, medals, and interactive activities where you could play against animated versions of some of the best goalies and shooters in the game. Admission rates go as follows, although they are subject to change:

| General Admission | $20.00 |

Youth (Ages 4-13)	$14.00
Senior (Ages 65 and Up)	$16.00
Children (Ages 3 and Under)	Free Admission

Whirlpool Aero Car - If heights are not a problem for you, a cable car ride over the Niagara Falls will prove to be an once-in-a-lifetime, breathtaking experience that will forever be remembered with fondness. You will be suspended 200 feet above the water, seeing everything from an unparalleled viewpoint.

When you're ready, take an hour and a half drive, or 85 miles to Niagara Falls and the mid-point of this trip. This is an iconic destination, and there is no shortage of things to do in this area. Plus it serves as a great staging ground for visiting Toronto and other points of this trip. Of course, you'll want to visit the iconic Niagara Falls, and some of the best ways involve the previously mentioned underground Journey behind the Falls and the Aero Car.

Suggested RV Park-1 in Niagara Falls

At this mid-point, you may want to stop and truly absorb your surroundings without any rush. There are two wonderful places to stay. The first is Campark Resorts Family Camping and RV Resort. Located in Niagara Falls, it is open April 15th to October 31st with an average rate of $53 to $75 per night. It is a pet-friendly park.

There are 350 sites with the following amenities:

- ☐ ATM Machines
- ☐ Ice
- ☐ Restaurant
- ☐ Restrooms
- ☐ Showers
- ☐ RV Supplies
- ☐ Snack Bar
- ☐ RV Service
- ☐ Laundry
- ☐ Groceries

- ☐ Heated Pool
- ☐ Horseshoes
- ☐ Playground
- ☐ Mini Golf
- ☐ Hot Tub
- ☐ Recreational Hall
- ☐ Pedal Carts
- ☐ Game Room
- ☐ Golf

SUGGESTED RV PARK-2 IN NIAGARA FALLS

Another option in Niagara Falls is Yogi Bear's Jellystone Park Camp-Resort. It is open May 1st to October 15th with an average rate of $53 to $93 each night. It is pet-friendly with restrictions on quantity and breed.

There are 146 sites with the following amenities:

- ☐ Internet
- ☐ Ice
- ☐ ATM Machines
- ☐ Snack Bar
- ☐ Restrooms

- ☐ Showers
- ☐ RV Supplies
- ☐ Groceries
- ☐ Laundry
- ☐ RV Service
- ☐ Heated Pool
- ☐ Horseshoes
- ☐ Playground
- ☐ Recreational Hall
- ☐ Game Room
- ☐ Mini Golf
- ☐ Pedal Carts

The last leg of the trip is only 22 minutes away and a short 19 miles to Fort Erie. Located on the banks of Lake Erie, this old fort played a role in some of the major battles of the War of 1812.

You can take expert guided tours of the area and learn about the importance of the site. You can also enjoy various hands-on exhibits that allow you to take part in history.

RV Camping at National Parks in Ontario

Bruce Peninsula National Park. Here you can spend hours hiking woodland trails replete with ancient Cedar trees, or take a swim in fresh, clean waters. From your RV you can also enjoy beautiful night skies stretched right above you. Bring a telescope with you in order to locate a few constellations, or visit during a predicted meteor shower for extra remarkable experience.

Georgian Bay Islands National Park. Home to the largest freshwater archipelago in the world, you can do anything from mountain biking, going for a dive in Lake Huron, fish or paddle, or hike one of the many ecosystems of this park. If you want a break from your RV, then consider renting one of the many well-furnished, cozy wooden cabins for a romantic getaway.

Point Pelee National Park. This is the second smallest national park in Canada, but it is the most diverse. The diverse habitats in this park are home to plants and animals that you won't see anywhere else in Canada, such as waves of Monarch butterflies, coyotes, the endangered Acadian flycatcher, wild turkeys, the fox snake, the five-lined skink, martens, and nine Carolinian floral species.

Pukaskwa National Park. Perfect place if you are in the mood for analyzing the rich geological opportunities with the hopes of finding precious stones and gems, picking through bunches of blueberry bushes, observing moose or black bears, going for a walk on secluded beaches, trying out the main coastal paddling route, exploring the backcountry hiking trails, or perhaps testing your courage on a suspension bridge atop a waterfall. The forest gives way to wetlands, lakes, and coastal regions as well.

Rouge National Urban Park. This park features natural, cultural, and agricultural landscapes. You'll be able to tour some of the last working farms in the Greater Toronto Area. It is home to the only campground in Toronto and one of the largest unspoiled marshes with a Carolinian ecosystem.

Thousand Islands National Park. Between the Canadian Shield and the Adirondack Mountains, you'll find this transition zone. Boating, paddling, and kayaking are popular activities here. Located just a few hours from Toronto or Montreal.

PRINCE EDWARD ISLAND

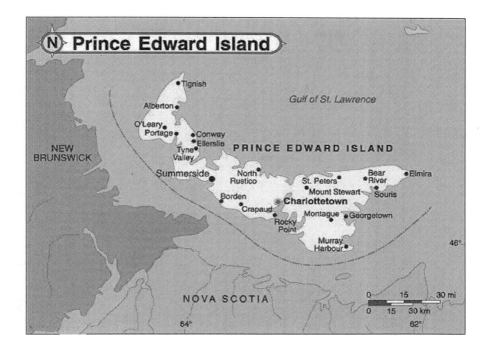

Located in the Gulf of St. Lawrence off the Atlantic Coast, Prince Edward Island is the smallest Canadian province. The island is no more than 139 miles long and between four and 40 miles wide. The northern shores are white sandy beaches with a gentle rolling landscape inland and red sandstone cliffs at the southern end. There are two main cities: Summerside and the capital of Charlottetown.

Climate-wise, the springs are comfortable with late May and early June being peak visiting times. Temperatures at this time often range from 50 to 70 degrees Fahrenheit. Summers can be hot but often aren't humid with daytime temperature averaging 70 degrees. Winters are cool with temperatures ranging from 30 to 10 degrees.

SUGGESTED RV TRIP

Due to the small size of this island, it isn't hard to see it within a single trip. However, whether you combine a drive on this island with another trip or simply want to stay somewhere rural for a few nights; there is still an RV trip well worth your time. It is only 61 miles and takes a little over an hour.

Start your trip in the cultural hub on the west side of the island at Summerside. Most activities here revolve around the water. There are a waterfront boardwalk and the parallel Water Street where you can see a handful of attractions that show how the province grew during the 19th century. Be sure to walk through the mock fishing village at Spinnakers

Landing, as well as checking out the following destinations:

- Harbourfront Theatre - Operating since 1996, this theatre is known for being a host to fantastic magic shows, opera and ballet performances, concerts, plays, public forums, and conferences. Visit and make sure you check their websites for the event dates so you can plan to arrive accordingly.

- The Confederation Trail - An abandoned railway now used as a walking and cycling trail during the summer as well as a snowmobile trail during the winter. It covers waterside communities, accommodations, restaurants, and markets to explore as you are walking or cycling across the island.

- Orwell Corner Historic Village - With crossroads established back in the 1890s, you can learn about what life was like during those days through educational programs, a visit to the blacksmith shop, a picnic outside a schoolhouse, or spending a day in the farm looking after friendly animals such as a cow, a few sheep, feeding pigs, and collecting eggs from the hens. Prices are prone to vary, but as of the year this guide was written, they are along the lines of:

Adults	$10.30
Students (Ages 6-8)	$5.18
Seniors	$9.25
Families (Two Adults, Two Children)	$28.75

- Eptek Art and Culture Center - A homey building that hosts exhibits about history and art that vary every season. It is always worthwhile to visit during the winter months since you will be invited to watch a travel film every week, or perhaps you might participate in their book club.

- Green Park Shipbuilding Museum and Yeo House - The island used to be based on shipbuilding during the Victorian era. It is quite interesting to learn about the rich history of a town while being surrounded by beautiful forests, flowers, and the coastline at a distance.

The Indian Head Lighthouse - First thought of in 1878, and first opened for navigation in 1881; the Indian Head Lighthouse is a remarkable 42-foot tall structure that was awarded a Provincial Designated Heritage Plaque and Certificate in 2013.

Your next stop is in Cape Egmont, a short 18-minute drive of less than a half hour. The main attraction here for tourists is the three Bottle Houses. These houses were completed in 1984 and are made from recycled bottles. Nearby you can also check out the Cape Egmont lighthouse.

Finish your trip in West Point, a short 43 miles and just short of an hour drive from Cape Egmont. This is a small and secluded town that is off-the-grid, which places you close to the Cedar Dunes Provincial Park. Here, you can enjoy your time on pristine beaches or in a wooded ecosystem accessed by the boardwalk and interpretive trails.

One of the most visited attractions is the West Point Lighthouse that was built in 1875 and is the tallest lighthouse on Prince Edward Island. Or perhaps the Canadian Potato Museum is more up to your speed. Worry not, it is not just all potatoes. Instead, it has one of the largest exhibits and collections of farm-related equipment and machinery used for growing and harvesting potatoes.

SUGGESTED CITY VISIT

No trip to Prince Edward Island is complete without at least stopping at Charlottetown. This Oceanside community is considered to be the birthplace of Canada and is the famed location of the novel, Anne of Green Gables. Visiting this town is necessary for anyone that wants to celebrate history.

In July and August, a walk through the historic district includes actors who tell the story of the forefathers through daily reenactments. The Confederation Center of the Arts deals with the moment in which the early founders gathered in 1867 to make Canada a country.

Stroll along Peake's Wharf to see the area from the point of view of the first settlers, then take a cruise in the harbor. Other attractions include the Province House Mansion, Victoria Park, St. Dunstan's Basilica Cathedral, Beaconsfield Historic House, St. Peter's Anglican Cathedral, and the Ardgowan National Historic Site.

RV Camping at National Parks in Prince Edward Island

Prince Edward Island National Park. Ardgowan is the former home of William Henry Pope, one of the Fathers of Confederation during the Charlottetown Conference of 1864. Today you can walk through the grounds surrounding this cottage-style house.

QUEBEC

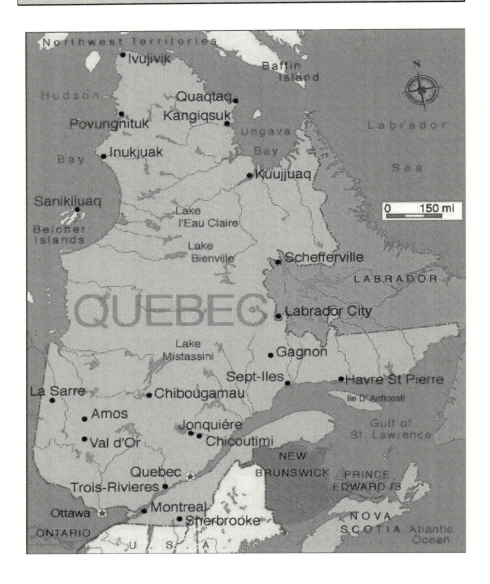

This province stretches from the US border to the Arctic Ocean and is between New Brunswick to the west and Labrador to the east. Due to this large expanse, there is a variety of landscapes to explore, from the plains in the north to the Appalachian Mountains in the south. There are also over a million lakes and over a thousand rivers. Montreal is the largest city and also the capital of Quebec.

There are three types of climates in Quebec: above the 58th parallel is the Arctic, the subarctic exists between the 50th and 58th parallel, and south of the 50th parallel there is a humid continental sort of weather. In the southern area of Quebec, there are four different seasons with temperature variations. In the winter, the average snowfall is over ten feet, so make sure you come prepared with winter clothes and snowshoes.

SUGGESTED RV TRIP

The best RV trip to take in Quebec is to follow the St. Lawrence River. Stop and take a kayak or canoe trip along the river or simply enjoy the examples of 1700s structures that dot the river bank. The total trip is 168 miles and takes about three hours. Let's look at it in greater detail.

Start your trip off in Montreal, and tread upon the cobblestone streets of Old Montreal to step back in time. Pay a visit to the Notre Dame Basilica and the Bonsecours Market with its silver domes. Place Jacque-Cartier's has been popular since colonial times and is a must-visit in the summer, being the entrance to the Old Port.

Head to the Old Park along the St. Lawrence River and take a panoramic cruise or even whitewater rafting. A short ferry ride away is the Parc Jean-Drapeau amusement park, gardens, and the Casino de Montreal. Some other places to consider are:

- **Mount Royal** - A beautiful outdoors location to relax, walk your pup, jog, go on a bike ride, or just get away from the world in an efficient manner for your own personal nature retreat.

- **Montreal Museum of Fine Arts** - It is the largest museum in the city with its photography exhibitions, architectural designs, and art pieces in both canvas and 3D forms. Admission prices will range from time to time, but for the most part, the general guideline goes as follows:

Age	Major Exhibitions	The Collections and Discovery Exhibitions
Ages 31 and Up	$23.00	$15.00
Ages 13 to 30	$15.00	Free
Ages 12 and Under (Must Be Accompanied By An Adult)	Free	Free
Wednesday Evenings (At 5 P.M)	$11.50	Closed

First Sunday of Each Month	Regular Fees	Free

- **Biosphere Environmental Museum** - For fans of science and the environment, you are now able to see this museum to understand more about water, air, climate change, biodiversity, sustainable development, and other major environmental issues through interactive activities and events. As always, the rates are prone to change, but as of this year, they are:

Adults	$15.00
Seniors (Ages 65 and Over)	$12.00
Students (Ages 18 and Over)	$10.00
Ages 17 and Under	Free

- **Montreal Insectarium** - Not all creepy critters are creepy! In fact, plenty of them are lovely to look at and fascinating to learn about. With a vast array of ants, butterflies, beetles, praying mantises, spiders, grasshoppers, and so, so many more, chances are you will find at least a dozen of these insects and bugs to be as iridescent as a precious jewel.

- **Mary Queen of The World Cathedral** - The third largest church in the whole of Quebec, and built at the end of the 19th century. It is a replica of the magnificent St. Peter's Basilica in Rome, covering almost 4,700 square meters in size. It is definitely a go-to if you are interested in history and architecture.

- **Jean Talon Market and the Atwater Market** - Both of these are separate farmers' markets, but they are as equally wonderful as can be. Fresh cheese from local Brown Swiss or Canadienne cows, vegetables, herbs, and fruits of all shapes and colors and sizes, pure maple syrup, raw apple or raspberry or blueberry honey, handmade ceramic creations, artisanal breads, cured salted meat, fresh seafood, eggs from local organic-based farms, desserts and chocolates, all of these and much more may be found at either location.

- **Cap-Saint-Jacques Nature Park** - Considered the largest park in Montreal, it is equipped with an ecological farm, a beach, a forest, and a picnic area, all surrounded by untamed wilderness. You could go ice skating, fishing, farming, swimming, kayaking, paddle-boarding, cycling, snowshoeing, hiking, or even on a horse-drawn sleigh ride if you so wish it. There are more modernized services such as free wireless and a sugar shack along with a snack bar, but as a whole, it is a great place to explore.

Take a drive about an hour and a half, 88 miles down the road to Trois-Rivieres. Located on the northern shore of the St. Lawrence River, this town was originally founded in 1634. Most of the main landmarks and sights in this town can be seen by walking down the main street of Boulevard des Forges. Some of those sights include:

- **La Vieille Prison de Trois-Rivières** - If you have ever wanted to visit a prison from the 19th century, we have found your spot. This antique prison may not be accessible for children younger than 12 years of age, but older visitors will be able to have a glimpse of what being a prisoner in this region was like.

- **Borealis Museum** - Paper, paper, paper. Check out the history of Canada's role in their previous paper company, as well as the lumberjacks, log drivers, and other workers who developed the company as the years went by.

- **Saint-Quentin Island** - After its deforestation in 1645, the island was used for agricultural purposes for almost 300 years until the 1930s, when people swam right onto the beach to relax. In 1961 the residents opted to construct a bridge between the beach and Highway 138 so that it was easier to access. After that point, the beach was closed for a few years due to pollution from the paper industry but has successfully reopened more than a decade ago, becoming a booming tourist attraction and key destination.

- **Museum of World Religions** - A worthwhile visit in order to understand more about the five main religions in the world. Learning about something you may not have previously known not only helps create a better-informed world but also makes room for tolerance and friendship. The detail here is that the main tours are in French.

End your trip with an hour and a half drive of 80 miles down the road to Quebec City. This city started as a fort overlooking the river in 1535. Today, the city still looks like the Old World, while offering all the amenities of a modern city.

It is the only place in North America outside of Mexico that still has the original walls from several 16th-century buildings and structures standing. In fact, there are nearly three miles of walls and gates to walk and see, as well as any of these attractions and destinations:

- **Épicerie J.A. Moisan** - Visit the oldest grocery store in North America, founded in 1871. It contains fine cheeses, hams, a Roaring Twenties and 30's decoration style (along with music playing in the background), and amazing products and food at an international scale. The store is typically open from Monday to Saturday, from 8:30am to 9pm, and on Sundays from 10am to 7pm.

- **Parc du Bois-de-Coulonge** - A beautiful 24 hectares all over Quebec, this park is brimming with forests, lakes and ponds, historic buildings (a gazebo, the lieutenant governor's house), blooming flower gardens. There sometimes are wildlife and plant observation tours in French, as well as restaurants, a picnic area, and a sugar shack on the premises. Pets are certainly allowed so long as they are well-behaved and preferably on a leash.

- **Baie De Beauport** - Similar to an open market, the bay of Beauport is an excellent location for events such as outdoor concerts, friendly sports games, picnics, strolls, a swim in the ocean, or simply having a lovely lunch before heading over to downtown Quebec City.

- **Parc des Chutes-de-la-Chaudière** - With the main attraction being a 114.83-foot tall waterfall that flows onto the St. Lawrence River, you can only guess how magnificent the view is from their suspension footbridge, or in any of the lookout points you reach after following a trail. Other activities could be to go on a bike riding adventure with varying degrees of difficulty, hiking, or fishing (with a license). Admission is free, and the park is open from early May to the end of October.

- **Hotel de Glace** - If you are the sort of person who prefers cold weather over warm, the Ice Hotel is definitely a must-see. It changes themes every winter, but it still consists of incredibly strong ice sculptures and structures holding the building together. You may construct your own glass made of ice, then drink a hearty cocktail out of it after a guided tour throughout the building.

- **Vieux Port** - Translated to the Old Port, there are fantastic shops, restaurants, views of the ice floating down the St. Lawrence River, it is a worthwhile location to visit if you do not have a set schedule or a set plan, and only wish to explore the city in its full rustic, astounding glory from up close.

- **Carnaval de Quebec** - Dubbed as the first major winter carnival formed back in 1894, the carnival began as an idea to bring morale and joy back to people's lives during harsh winters. Typically it consists of 10 days' worth of activities, festivals, food, fundraisers, contests, and live musical performances.

- **Quartier Petit-Champlain** - Boasting 45 boutiques and restaurants open year-round, Quartier Petit-Champlain is a street with old buildings that covers any type of shopping interest you would like, from body care (bath bombs, artisanal soaps, handmade shampoos) to sweets and craftsmen creations.

RV Camping at National Parks in Quebec

Forillon National Park. At this national park, you can get out on the water and paddle with the seals while watching whales pass; a very unique experience. You can also take a walk through the forest and perhaps see some beavers at work. Other suggestions cover snorkeling, bird-watching, strolling across the gentle crackle of a pebble beach. The cheapest admission fees can be obtained from either the month of June or from early September to early October.

La Mauricie National Park. This park offers multiple outdoor activities with hills, forests, and more than 150 lakes and streams to explore. You can visit this park at any time of the year, weather permitting.

Mingan Archipelago National Park Reserve. You could go on a stroll amidst large monolith formations, or catch a glimpse of a few whales or seals in any of the 1,000 islands and islets composing the archipelago. This park is the definition of remote. It is the furthest you can get from the crowds and city life. This is the best place to get away from it all to watch marine and bird life, such as the friendly puffin.

SASKATCHEWAN

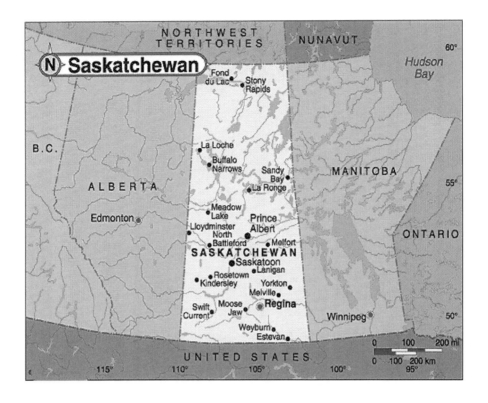

Saskatchewan is one of the Canadian Prairie Provinces with Manitoba to the east and Alberta to the west. The name comes from the Plains Indian word "kisiskāciwani-sīpiy" that means a swift flowing river. Therefore, Saskatchewan is the name of the major river system flowing through the province. The largest city in the province is Saskatoon while the capital is Regina.

The summers in this province are typically warm and dry with high temperatures of about 60 degrees Fahrenheit in May and then about 90 to 100 degrees Fahrenheit in July and August. However, the nights always tend to be cooler.

The winter months are cold and dry, typically starting in November and going until spring starts in April; during this time the temperatures tend to remain below the freezing point. Saskatchewan gets the most sun of all Canadian provinces, with 2,000 to 2,500 hours of sun a year.

SUGGESTED CITY VISIT

A suggested RV drive would take you along the Yellowhead Highway that we've already discussed. If you have more time to spend in the province, then I suggest you head to Saskatoon and spend a few days at a nearby RV park and explore the city in detail. Let's look at what a visit to the city would entail.

Saskatoon has more days of sun per year than nearly all other Canadian cities, as we have covered. The city also features a downtown area with a vibrant and diverse cultural scene replete with natural beauty. This is an active and welcoming city that deserves a few days to fully explore.

If you want to venture into the outdoors, then head to the Meewasin Valley along the border of the South Saskatchewan River as it flows through the downtown part of the city. The Meewasin Trail is over 40 miles and takes you through forests and along the river with many smaller paths to take side adventures.

Take a short half hour drive to the south of the city, and you'll come to Blackstrap Lake and Brightwater Reservoir. Here you'll find excellent fishing opportunities for walleye. If you don't like fishing, it is also an excellent destination for boating and swimming.

For the sports fan, head over to the Wyant Group Raceway on the north side of the city. In late July, this raceway is home to the Pinty's Series and features two days of stock car races.

History buffs can step back in time and learn the history of the diverse cultural traditions in Saskatoon by going to the Western Development Museum. This is the largest human history museum in the province, with over 75,000 artifacts displayed as living history exhibits.

SUGGESTED RV PARK-1 IN SASKATOON

If you choose to stay in the Saskatoon area for a few days, there are a couple of good options. The first of these is the Campland RV Resort. It is open April 4th to November 1st with an average rate of $42 to $46 per night. It is a pet-friendly park with restrictions on quantity.

It has 132 sites and features the following amenities:

- ☐ Internet
- ☐ Laundry
- ☐ Ice
- ☐ Restrooms

- ☐ RV Supplies
- ☐ Groceries
- ☐ Showers
- ☐ Heated Pool
- ☐ Playground

SUGGESTED RV PARK-2 IN SASKATOON

Another option is the Gordon Howe Campground. It is open April 16th to October 14th with an average rate of $38 to $46 per night. It is also a pet-friendly park.

There are 135 sites with the following amenities:

- ☐ Internet
- ☐ Ice
- ☐ ATM Machines
- ☐ Groceries
- ☐ Restrooms
- ☐ Showers
- ☐ RV Supplies
- ☐ Laundry
- ☐ Playground

RV Camping at National Parks in Saskatchewan

Grasslands National Park. This is the best place to see dinosaur fossils and take a trip way back in time. You'll also see tipi rings that are remnants of First Nations communities. More recent history can be found in the ruins of homesteads from when settlers tried to tame the prairie.

Prince Albert National Park. An accessible wilderness option with plenty of outdoor activities within the central part of the province. Hike through forests, canoe in lakes, and view free-roaming bison. Stay in the nearby town of Waskesiu if you need a few days and want to be closer to civilization.

YUKON

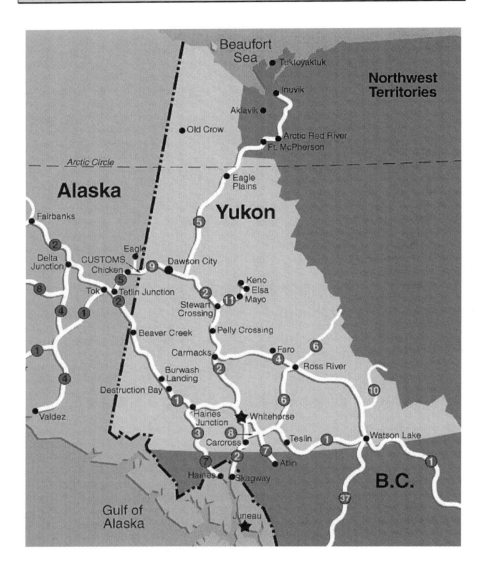

Canada's tallest peak can be found in the Yukon province. It is also home to the largest non-polar ice fields, several Heritage Rivers, and an abundant range of wildlife. The province is about the same size as the state of California, but with a far smaller number of population. Nearly 80 percent of the land in this province consists of wilderness, offering you a unique outdoor experience and a sense of comfortable solitude.

The weather in this province can vary. You may even get to experience all four seasons in a single day. In the summer, the sun can shine from dusk until dawn with temperatures about 80 to 90 degrees Fahrenheit. In winter, the temperature can easily drop to minus 20 degrees Fahrenheit.

Suggested City Visit

An RV road trip in the Yukon takes you on the path to Alaska from Alberta. If you enjoy the wilderness views out your windows, then take the time to spend a few days in Yukon before heading back on the road to Alaska. The best place to visit is Whitehorse, a town which you may remember from an earlier mention.

Just for the recap, and to perhaps spark your interest in the area once more: The town of Whitehorse holds the Guinness World Record for least polluted air. This is a great destination for outdoor activities such as dog-sled travels or viewing the northern lights. Whitehorse is a small, but a bustling town that was first established during the Klondike Gold Rush in the 1890s. Later, a major railroad was routed through the city and today both the Klondike and Alaska Highways travel to the town that is the capital of the province.

The downtown area of Whitehorse offers a quaint and colorful spot to hang out for a while. There are multiple trails you can hike that will take you along the Yukon River and through woodlands. If you are traveling when the weather is nice, then you can canoe or kayak along the water. Consider hiking Miles Canyon to get an aerial view of the rock formations along the Yukon River. Walk across a suspension bridge over the river.

There are abundant wildlife species in the Yukon wilderness. At the Whitehorse Fishway, you can observe wild salmon as they travel from the Bering

Sea 2,000 miles to their spawning grounds. You can also visit the Yukon Wildlife Preserve which allows you to explore 700 acres of natural landscape and the variety of animals that call it home. Whether you walk or take a bus tour, you have a chance to view moose, mountain goats, caribou, arctic foxes, and many other mammals.

If you want to head indoors for a little bit, then you should visit the MacBride Museum of Yukon History. Here you'll find a variety of artifacts and educational displays that discuss the history of the region. A popular activity for families is to pan for gold. You can also head to the Yukon Visitor Information Center to view a short movie about the area and learn about the best places to check out nearby.

RV Camping at National Parks in Yukon

Ivvavik National Park. This is the necessary destination for river rafters. The Firth River cuts through canyons and mountain valleys on its way to the Arctic Ocean. There is also a fly-in base camp that offers easy access to the surrounding Arctic landscape.

Kluane National Park and Reserve. This park features 17 to the 20 highest peaks in Canada, making it ideal for a mountain climber. It also has vast icefields and alpine scenery to enjoy on a leisure stroll. History buffs can see First Nation culture and history in the area as well.

Vuntut National Park. This park is in the northern area of the province and is the closest you can get to explore the untouched wilderness. While there learn about the Vuntut Gwitchin people and how they live in relation to the land and animals throughout the Yukon province.

Part – 2
Exploring Alaska

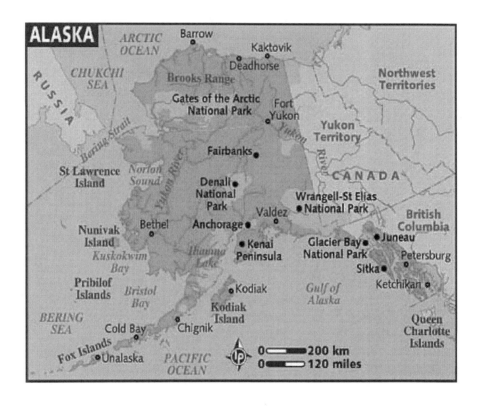

RV TRIP TO ALASKA

Alaska is possibly one of the most picturesque places in North America. When it comes to the United States, it is a great place to travel to get away from it all and simply take a breath of fresh air. There are breathtaking landscapes and laid back cities to visit.

For many good reasons, Alaska is on the top of many travelers' lists. It is a particularly good summer destination to escape the heat in the lower 48 states. Alaska is home to quite a few RV parks and campgrounds, all of them located in very scenic parts.

There are plenty of things to see and do in both cities and outdoors. Plus there are stunning National Parks such as Denali that are a must-visit. Let's look at what you need to do to be prepared for your trip to Alaska and what you should see during your stay.

THINGS YOU SHOULD KNOW

When it comes to traveling to Alaska, you need to be prepared to cross through Canada first. We've already discussed what you need to be prepared to cross the border. However, there are a few things you should know about Alaskan roadways before you try to drive an RV to and around Alaska.

First, all Alaskan highways have designated numbers as well as names; for example, the Richardson

Highways is also known as AK-4. When you need to ask about directions you should always refer to a road by its name rather than the route number. Otherwise it might lead to some confusion.

Since most people travel to Alaska in the summer, this is when most Alaskan roads are under construction. Therefore, be prepared for a lot of dust and rocky conditions when passing through these construction zones. Drive slowly in these sections and use your AC to avoid dust getting accumulated inside the RV.

Some road hazards that you should be aware of include frost heaves, soft shoulders, and potholes. Potholes are most frequent after winter before they have been filled by the Department of Transportation (DoT). If you need to pull over, make sure you do so on the steady ground.

Lastly, you ought to know that gas stations are few and far between throughout Alaska. This is why you want to carefully plan all your routes. You should intend to get at least 200 miles from a full tank of gas unless you want to find yourself stuck on the side of the road. With a combination of gas rationing and careful planning, you'll be able to get between gas stations and destinations with little to no problems.

Suggested Alaskan Bucket List

Depending on your outdoor skills and your interests you may have a varied list of things you want to do while in Alaska. However, there are a few main things that are on everyone's list when traveling to Alaska. Consider the list to help you get some ideas for what you want to do.

Copper River Salmon. Take the time to go fishing for this popular fish and then cook it fresh over an open fire while camping. There is nothing better than a hot meal, recently caught, in the company of great people and surrounded by trees and water.

Grizzly River Feeding. Watching the grizzly bears fish from the river in person is a wonderful opportunity, but make sure you keep a safe distance between you and the bear in case, otherwise there might be a bit of a bear-chasing incident.

Float Plane. Take off and land in the crystal clear waters of an Alaskan lake. In between, get to have a unique view of the Alaskan wilderness.

King Crab. Second, only to salmon, there's nothing better than fresh Alaskan king crab. Pull a trap from the bay waters if you're there during the season and enjoy a fresh crab while breathing in the fresh outdoor air.

Ice Climbing. This isn't for everyone since you'll need to be experienced at mountain and ice climbing before attempting this, but climbing a glacier can be a unique outdoor experience rarely done anywhere else in North America. The best option for this is Exit Glacier. Please have all the necessary equipment for this activity.

In addition, while you're in Alaska there are some specific species of wildlife you should try to get on camera:

- ☐ Puffins
- ☐ Wolves
- ☐ Orca
- ☐ Whales
- ☐ Polar Bear
- ☐ Arctic Fox
- ☐ Lynx

Now that you've started to get some ideas for your dream Alaska RV trip let's consider some ideal RV trips through parts of Alaska and things you should see.

SUGGESTED RV TRIP

The first trip is an adventure-filled journey for those who want to experience the outdoors. It takes you across the Kenai Peninsula from Anchorage to Homer in 331 miles. This drive across the last frontier takes about six and a half hours but should be broken up with a few stays along the way so you can see everything you want to see.

Start your trip in the city of Anchorage. Within the city limits alone there are about 250 miles of trails to hike. The pathways are paved and perfect for hiking, biking, and even horseback riding. Along these pathways, you are sure to come across some moose, nearly 1,500 of which are spread throughout the parks and green spaces in the city. Just 20 minutes from the downtown you'll find the Chugach Mountains, where you can do anything related to glaciers whether it be hiking, rafting, or fishing.

- Far North Bicentennial Park - 4,000 acres of wild, rugged landscapes teeming with bears every summer upon the return of salmon. A good precaution is to carry bear spray with you and do not venture too far from the main established trails and paths. Also avoid leaving a trail of food which will lead curious animals' right to you, whether you are prepared for them or not.

- Kenai Fjords National Park - You could kayak the crystal clear waters of the fjords, hike the difficult 8.2-mile round-trip that is the Harding Icefield Trail, participate in a ranger-led program, or stroll on to the Exit Glacier. The park is available for the most part, with a few attractions closed or restricted due to harsh weather conditions from time to time.

- Alaska Botanical Garden - Describing itself as an independent nonprofit living museum, the Alaska Botanical Garden displays the natural, colorful flora in Alaska, accompanied by friendly critters such as ladybirds, certain species of butterflies, and bugs.

- Hilltop Ski Area - For the more adrenaline-fueled soul, this ski area was first established in 1984 and consists of a chairlift, a handle tow, and 30 acres of skiing grounds that vary from difficult to easy. It is always a worthwhile visit if you want to try something new, or to brush up on an already-established skill.

- Alaska Zoo - An idea first cultivated in 1969, the Alaska Zoo includes 100 animals that were rescued or previously injured then cured back to perfect health but unable to be released back into the wild. Be prepared to walk quite a bit, since the zoo stretches across 25 acres of land on the Anchorage Hillside. You get black bears, seals, polar bears, moose, wolves, Canada Lynx, oxen, porcupines, tigers, and wolves.

- Alaska Native Heritage Center - If you have ever wanted to learn more about Alaska's indigenous people, such as their culture, their history, their language, and their stories, pay a visit to the museum and understand what it is all about.

Suggested RV Park in Anchorage

If you need to stay a few days to explore all that Anchorage has to offer then consider staying at the Anchorage Ship Creek RV Park. Open May 1st to September 30th with an average cost of $19 to $59 per night. It is a pet-friendly park.

There are 130 sites with the following amenities:

- ☐ Internet
- ☐ Ice
- ☐ Restrooms
- ☐ Showers
- ☐ Self-Service RV Wash
- ☐ Laundry

The next stop is less than an hour from Anchorage and is 48 miles on the Seward Highway to Portage. Here you must see the Portage Glacier that stands ten stories above the waters of Portage Lake.

Nearby, you should also stop by the Begich Boggs Nature Center where you can walk the five-mile Trail of Blue Ice path that takes you up close to glaciers and rivers filled with salmon. In Portage you can also visit the Alaska Wildlife Conservation Center that offers tours to help you glimpse rare mammals such as bears, moose, and musk oxen.

Your next stop is about an hour and a half away in Seward. The drive is 378 miles and takes you to the shores of Resurrection Bay. Here you can visit the Kenai Fjords, National Park. Seward has long been known as one of the more picturesque towns in Alaska.

In the downtown area, you can catch sight of a variety of shops and the harbor itself. From there you can take a water taxi to explore the coves and beaches in the bay where you have the chance to observe otters, harbor seals, and bald eagles.

You can also take boat tours of the Kenai Fjords National Park, where you can comfortably see whales, puffins, and playful sea lions. On land, take a ten-minute drive to Exit Glacier where you can hike a half-mile trail to the glacier.

Listen to the ice field crackle as it adjusts to the temperatures, and remember that sound with fondness in the years to come.

Less than an hour brings you to Cooper Landing. 48 miles down the road you'll find this town that was founded in the mid-1800s by gold prospectors and is now a great spot for those who want to view natural resources.

This is a great place for fishing along the several miles of the river's shore. Within the town, you'll find numerous outfitters and guide services that will help you plan your fishing adventure. Downstream, you also have the option of rafting rapids through the Kenai Canyon.

Another 56 miles and about an hour-long drive takes you to Kenai, the largest community on the Kenai Peninsula and a popular destination for outdoor activities. The city overlooks the mouth of the Kenai River and is a great spot for sport-fishing.

In fact, eight of the ten largest king salmon were caught in these waters. In the spring and early summer months, you should go to the Beluga Whale Lookout along the coastal bluff to view the whales.

SUGGESTED RV PARK IN KENAI

If you need somewhere to stay for a while, consider the Diamond M Ranch Resort. Open all year with an average rate of $53 to $95 per night. It is a pet-friendly park. There are 77 sites with the following amenities:

- ☐ Internet
- ☐ Ice
- ☐ Self-Service RV Wash
- ☐ Restrooms
- ☐ Showers
- ☐ Fishing Guides
- ☐ Fishing Supplies
- ☐ Laundry
- ☐ Horseshoes
- ☐ Recreational Hall
- ☐ Playground

The last portion of your trip is 81 miles and about an hour and a half to Homer. This is the spot where the locals go for vacation; a unique town is known as the Halibut Fishing Capital of the World. Downtown's

Pioneer Street is an excellent place for a unique stroll.

You can also take a water taxi across the bay to Kachemak Bay State Wilderness Park, a 350 thousand-acre park of glaciers, mountains, and coves. In other words, a great place for kayaking, backpacking, and camping. Be sure to visit the Homer Spit, a 4.5-mile long sliver of beach that sticks out into the bay.

SUGGESTED RV TRIP

Another RV trip worth taking when visiting Alaska is to travel Richardson Highway. This 383-mile stretch of road takes you from the water off Valdez to the interior beauty and ends at the bustling city of Fairbanks. The drive takes a little over 16 hours and is good for at least several days' worth of activities depending on what you choose to do.

You could start your trip at the beginning of the "Adventure Corridor" in the historic gold rush town of Valdez, located at the foot of the Chugach Mountains where the land meets the sea. There is plenty of seafood and wildlife along with many festivals. In Prince William Sound you have the opportunity to watch humpback whales breach.

Or you can spend your time watching puffins and bald eagles. Nearly everywhere you go here you can enjoy hiking, boating, wildlife-viewing, and fishing. You need to visit the iconic Columbia Glacier. There are also several accessible trails through the forests.

SUGGESTED RV PARK IN VALDEZ

If you need to spend a day or two to explore the surrounding area, then consider staying at the Eagles Rest RV Park & Cabins. Open May 15th to September 15th with an average rate of $39 to $54 per night. This is a pet-friendly park.

There are 197 sites with the following amenities:

- ☐ Internet
- ☐ RV Supplies
- ☐ Groceries
- ☐ Metered Gas

- ☐ Self-Service RV Wash
- ☐ Restrooms
- ☐ Showers
- ☐ Firewood
- ☐ Restaurant
- ☐ Fishing Guides
- ☐ Fishing Supplies
- ☐ Laundry
- ☐ Ice
- ☐ Cable
- ☐ Horseshoes
- ☐ Frisbee Golf

Your next stop is Glennallen, about a two hour and 121-mile drive up the highway. This route takes you through the Copper River Valley. Once there Glennallen serves as the gateway to Wrangell-St. Elias National Park and Preserve.

This park is nearly 13 million acres and is the largest park managed by the US National Park Service. It features some of the tallest mountain peaks in the nation, and the wilderness it contains is home to animals such as the trumpeter swan, caribou, and Copper River salmon.

Next stop is Summit Lake, about five hours and 257 miles down the road. This crystal clear lake was carved by glaciers long ago. In April there is a contest to see who is faster, a skier or a snowmobile. In late summer, the lake is populated with Copper River salmon who have come upstream to spawn in Gunn Creek.

Access to the lake is easy since it is right next to the highway — definitely the place to go if you want to fish or just to observe this species more closely.

Your longest drive is about seven and a half hours or 410 miles to Delta Junction. This area was popular during the Chisana Gold Strike of 1913, and the town has changed several times since then. In the 1920s the town was chosen for the buffalo importation program, and today the town features the 90,000 acre Delta Bison Sanctuary. The Sullivan Roadhouse Historical Museum preserves the oldest roadhouse in the Alaskan interior.

End your trip in Fairbanks by driving about two hours and 95 miles. This town is known as the Land of the Midnight Sun. It started in the Gold Rush and today hosts the Yukon Quest a 1,000-mile dog--sledding race. In summertime, daylight never ends and the Midnight Sun Festival starts, which includes a midnight baseball game.

A short two hours away is Denali National Park so you can explore the wilderness as well. If you travel in August or April, you can also end your trip by viewing the Aurora Borealis.

Suggested RV Park in Fairbanks

If you need to spend a little time in this area or if you just aren't ready to leave yet, consider staying at the Riverview RV Park. Open May 15th to September 15th with an average rate of $43 to $55 per night. The park is pet-friendly.

There are 160 sites with the following amenities:

- ☐ Internet
- ☐ ATM Machine
- ☐ Cable
- ☐ Fishing Supplies
- ☐ RV Supplies
- ☐ Restrooms
- ☐ Showers
- ☐ Ice
- ☐ Self-Service RV Wash
- ☐ Laundry
- ☐ Groceries
- ☐ Fishing Guides
- ☐ Recreational Hall
- ☐ Driving Range
- ☐ Putting Green
- ☐ Golf
- ☐ Horseshoes

Suggested RV Trip

If you have more time to spend in Alaska consider an extended trip that takes you to several points along the two trips above and much more to see all the highlights that Alaska has to offer. Let's look at this extended trip.

Start your trip at the stunning Denali National Park. When visiting the Last Frontier, you will most likely want to enjoy the actual panoramic opportunities, which is fantastic news since this national park is six million acres of excellent views. Denali is open year-round, but the peak time to visit is from late May until early September.

Since most private vehicles aren't allowed on the roads in the park, you can choose to enjoy it by bus or helicopter. No matter how you explore the park, you're likely to see bears, moose, and caribou. If you want some guidance on your trip, then take a ranger-led hiking tour. Also visit the on-site kennels where you can see the Denali sled dogs, one of the main attractions of this park.

It costs $10 per person to get into Denali National Park and children under 15 years of age are free admission. The fee gets you seven days within the park.

There are three campgrounds in the park open to RVs: Riley Creek Campground, Savage River Campground, and Teklanika River Campground. Savage River and Teklanika River are only open in the summer, and none of the campgrounds can accommodate RVs over 40 feet. If you need to stay outside the park, the closest RV Park is Denali Rainbow Village and McKinley RV and Campground, with 50 campsites with full hookups for RVs.

From Denali take a drive to the North Pole, Alaska where you should visit the Santa Claus House. Whether you celebrate Christmas or not, there is a lot to enjoy in this small town just south of Fairbanks, Alaska. The town was founded in 1953 and only has about 2,000 residents.

At the Santa Claus House, you can feed live reindeer and tread around 9,000 square feet of shopping. A nearby place to stay is the Riverview RV Park on the

Chena River, where you can find 160 full hookup sites with on-site laundry. You can also head into Fairbanks where there is no shortage of campgrounds to stay at with your RV.

Your next stop is in Sutton, Alaska for the Matanuska Glacier Hike. While there are plenty of glaciers to see and hike in Alaska, this is the largest glacier in the United States accessible by vehicle at 24 miles in length. You can book a guided tour of the glacier through Matanuska Glacier Adventures of Alaska at $100 for a once in a lifetime experience.

You can also pay $30 for unguided access and hike through the glacier yourself. Just be sure to dress in your warmest clothes before venturing out onto the glacier, and always respect the environment by never littering, feeding the wildlife, or marking any of the stones or ice formations in any way, shape, or form.

After a long day of hiking the glacier, you can stay at the nearby Grand View Cafe and RV Park. There are only 25 sites here, and it is open from May to September. Otherwise, you can choose to stay at

Pinnacle Mountain RV Park which is open throughout the year with an on-site grocery store and restaurant.

No trip to Alaska is complete without stopping in Fairbanks to view the Northern Lights or the Aurora Borealis. Most people choose to travel to Alaska in the warm summer months, but smart travelers know to visit after September since the Northern Lights are best viewed in the late fall, winter, and early spring.

The best place to view these lights is in Fairbanks where you'll see the sky lit up in beautiful shades of blue, green, yellow, and red. Best of all it is something you can do for free from the comfort of your RV campsite.

There is no shortage of RV places to stay in and around the Fairbanks area. An excellent option is River's Edge RV Park with 167 sites with both full and basic hookups. Another option is the Chena River Wayside RV Park with 56 RV sites. You can also stay at the state-run campground with 26 acres of scenic woodland along the river to explore.

Your next stop is at Totem Bight State Historic Park in Borough, Alaska (just north of Ketchikan, Alaska). This park started out in 1938 as the US Forest Service started to restore dozens of totem poles abandoned by the Native Americans. Eventually, they created the replicas you can now view at the park. At this park, you'll also be able to learn about the cultures of the Tlingit and Haida Indians while enjoying nature and the ocean.

The best option for staying with your RV near Ketchikan is the Clover Pass Resort. Here you have full hookups with coin laundry and a shuttle that takes you to nearby attractions. The resort also offers fishers the chance to catch salmon and halibut on-site. There are also boat rentals for those who want to get out on the water at a reasonable price.

Next stop is the Alaska Wildlife Conservation Center in Portage. This can be an excellent stop, especially if you have kids. But it is also enjoyable for adults, so worry not. The center covers 200 acres and seeks out to educate the public about the wildlife that resides in the state. In addition, it is a sanctuary that cares for injured and orphaned wildlife such as bison, black bears, eagles, deer, and foxes.

Throughout the week you can view free animal programs that show how the center nurses animals back to health and continues to care for them well into their adulthood if they cannot return to the wild. The park costs $15 for adults, $10 for kids aged 7 to 17, and free for children under six.

Just four minutes from the center you'll find the Portage Valley RV Park, the only campground in the area that offers electric and water for RVs. After this, you'll need to travel at least 20 minutes to the Bird Creek Motel and RV Park where you'll find eight sites with power and water.

When gold was discovered in northwest Canada in 1896, many men started to travel north, raising the number to approximately 100,000 people coming through Skagway. It was here that most of those men stocked up on supplies, equipment, and food in order to survive in the Last Frontier.

Later, Skagway became a ghost town when the boom dried up, yet the historic downtown area was preserved by the National Park Service. Whether you are interested in history or simply want to stop while passing through, visit the Klondike Gold Rush National Park. While there, take a guided tour of the downtown sections and hike the Chilkoot Trail. If you are short on time at least head to the visitors' center and look at the interactive exhibits.

Just a block away from the park you can stay at the Pullen Creek RV Park. There are 34 gravel sites and 12 harbor sites where you can have both water and electric hookups. Another option within walking distance to the historic Skagway district is the Garden City, RV Park.

Next up on your trip is the Homer Spit. This four and a half-mile piece of land sticks out into the Kachemak Bay. It may not sound like much, but it is a top spot to visit on many people's list. From the boat harbor, you can enjoy breathtaking views of the glacier-topped mountains and smooth water for miles on end.

There's plenty to do at the Homer Spit whether it be shopping, boating, hiking, or fishing. If you choose to fish, there are even several restaurants in the area that will offer to cook the fish you caught during the day. The town of Homer is also known as the arts capital of Alaska so you'll want to be sure to visit a few galleries in order to confirm that reputation for yourself. Lastly, make sure you drive 23 miles north to Anchor Point; this is the westernmost point in the United States and is accessible by road.

The city of Homer runs their own RV Park that is open from April 1st to October 30th and is available on a first come, first served basis. If you can't find a space here, then head to the Alaska Heritage RV Park next to a famous fishing hole. This RV Park has full hookups, free internet, coin laundry, a private beach, and even its own espresso bar. Talk about luxury camping.

The second to the last stop is at the Chena Hot Springs near Fairbanks. This will give you a chance to warm up after enjoying the cold outdoors. The water temperature here averages 106 degrees

Fahrenheit year-round. It is quite amazing to dip in warm water while visiting one of the coldest places in the world.

The steam and minerals in the water is believed to have healing properties, so it cannot possibly hurt to check it out. If you want to cool down after a warm soak, then you can visit the Chena Hot Springs Resort's Aurora Ice Museum. Here you can view ice sculptures from two world champion ice carvers Steve and Heather Brice. End the day relaxing at the Aurora Ice Bar. It costs $15 to visit the springs and the Aurora Ice Museum.

The spring has 24 campsites available from May 15th to September 15th. There are no electric or plumbing hookups, but there is drinking water and a dump station available. A nearby option is the Northern-Moosed RV Park and Campground that offers both full and partial hookup sites. Another option is the Riverview RV Park with 160 full hookup sites that can accommodate RVs over 70 feet. Lastly, there is the "C" Lazy Moose RV Park that has full hookups, laundry facilities, and internet.

End your trip in Juneau, Alaska with a visit to the Alaskan Brewing Company. This is the oldest brewery in Alaska and was founded in 1986 by Marcy and Geoff Larson.

Today, the company brews seven beers year-round with eight rotating seasonal and limited edition beers. The tasting room is open year-round, and for $20 you can have a guided tour that comes with seven samples. Nearby there is the pet-friendly Spruce Meadow RV Park with 47 full hookup sites and internet. Another option is the Auke Bay RV Park which is also pet-friendly and features electric and water hookups.

RV Camping at Alaska State Parks

Alaska is home to 3.3 million acres of state park lands. Most state parks are primitive and only occasionally have water available. Alaska is a place where even RV travel comes with some rough outdoor living. Some basics to know:

☐ Typical Cost: Free to $15

- Water: Rarely
- Electric: Rarely
- Sewer: No
- Most have a 15-night maximum stay.

The following are the state parks with RV campsites in Alaska:

- Chugach State Park - 171 sites: some with water
- Big Delta State Historical Park - 23 sites with water
- Clearwater State Recreation Site - 17 sites
- Delta State Recreation Site - 25 sites
- Donnelly Creek State Recreation Site - 12 sites
- Quartz Lake State Recreation Area - 103 sites
- Birch Lake State Recreation Site - 17 sites
- Chena River State Recreation Site - 60 sites, 11 with water and electric hookups
- Chena River State Recreation Area - RV sites
- Harding Lake State Recreation Area - 78 sites
- Lower Chatanika River State Recreational Area - 40 sites: water available
- Upper Chatanika River State Recreation Site - 24 sites: water available

- ☐ Salcha River State Recreation Site - 6 sites
- ☐ Eagle Trail State Recreation Site - 5 sites
- ☐ Moon Lake State Recreation Site - 15 sites
- ☐ Tok River State Recreation Site - 10 sites
- ☐ Crooked Creek State Recreation Site - 80 sites
- ☐ Johnson Lake State Recreation Area - 48 sites
- ☐ Ninilchik State Recreation Area - RV sites
- ☐ Fort Abercrombie State Historical Park - some sites can accommodate RVs
- ☐ Buskin River State Recreation Site - 15 sites

Pasagshak River State Recreation Site - 12 primitive sites

Now that you know what you can do in the Canadian and Alaskan wilderness you are probably anxious to hit the open road and have your next adventure. However, before you head out, I have a few final tips to share with you.

TRAVELING ON A BUDGET

TRIP BUDGET

DAY 1	Estimated	Actual	Difference
Gas			$ -
Food			$ -
Lodging			$ -
Entertainment			$ -
Misc.			$ -
DAY 1 Total	$ -	$ -	$ -

DAY 2	Estimated	Actual	Difference
Gas			$ -
Food			$ -
Lodging			$ -
Entertainment			$ -
Misc.			$ -
DAY 2 Total	$ -	$ -	$ -

DAY 3	Estimated	Actual	Difference
Gas			$ -
Food			$ -
Lodging			$ -
Entertainment			$ -
Misc.			$ -
DAY 3 Total	$ -	$ -	$ -

DAY 4	Estimated	Actual	Difference
Gas			$ -
Food			$ -
Lodging			$ -
Entertainment			$ -
Misc.			$ -
DAY 4 Total	$ -	$ -	$ -

DAY 5	Estimated	Actual	Difference
Gas			$ -
Food			$ -
Lodging			$ -
Entertainment			$ -
Misc.			$ -
DAY 5 Total	$ -	$ -	$ -

DAY 6	Estimated	Actual	Difference
Gas			$ -
Food			$ -
Lodging			$ -
Entertainment			$ -
Misc.			$ -
DAY 6 Total	$ -	$ -	$ -

DAY 7	Estimated	Actual	Difference
Gas			$ -
Food			$ -
Lodging			$ -
Entertainment			$ -
Misc.			$ -
DAY 7 Total	$ -	$ -	$ -

TOTAL	Estimated	Actual	Difference
Gas	$ -	$ -	$ -
Food	$ -	$ -	$ -
Lodging	$ -	$ -	$ -
Entertainment	$ -	$ -	$ -
Misc.	$ -	$ -	$ -
TOTAL	$ -	$ -	$ -

BOONDOCKING

Alaskan and Canadian highways are great places to boondock for those traveling in an RV. Most people who travel the highways are simply passing through, but there are some who camp or attempt to camp along the highway.

When traveling along the highway in Alaska or Canada, there isn't much need to pay for a campsite unless you need the hookups. So if you want to travel on a budget, then you need to boondock as many nights as possible. There are many pull outs where you are allowed to camp unless it is posted otherwise. Nearly 90 percent of pullouts allow at least one night of camping.

If you don't like the idea of pulling off the highway and spending the night, there are other options that provide a little more privacy. There aren't a lot of incorporated towns along the main highways, but if you find one you're likely to also quickly locate a better place to park. These spots would give you a more secluded space to spend the night before getting back on the road.

Travel in the Summer

It is best to travel to Canada and Alaska in the summer. While the main highways are plowed daily and accessible in winter, it will cost you more money to travel during this season. For one, there is more daylight if you are able to travel in the summer, so you can easily drive until ten o'clock at night and still have time to spare. In the winter, daylight hours are limited, and the roads can be difficult to drive at night due to harsh, unpredictable weather and roaming wildlife.

If you travel from October to April, then chains and/or snow tires are needed to drive over most passes. There will also be snow on the ground, which makes it more difficult to use boondocking to save money.

Essentially, you may end up spending more on hotels since many campsites and gas stations are closed in the winter months. You'll also be spending more on eating out since you won't be able to cook outside unless you intend to book a few local B&Bs.

STOCK UP WHEN STOPPING IN LARGE TOWNS

There are a few more populated towns with resources along the major highways in Canada and Alaska. These are the best places to do the bulk of your shopping. A few will even have a Walmart where you are able to spend the night. Larger cities with more resources mean that prices are lower since there is more competition.

You should also purchase gas in any larger town you travel through. If you get poor gas mileage, it is especially important that you carry extra gas with you.

Sometimes you can go long periods without finding a gas station, and some small towns may even be out of gas when you pass through. Don't run the risk of running out of gas since there is also limited cell service in between towns.

Avoid Using American Dollars in Canada

Most places in Canada will take the US dollar. This is convenient but doesn't save you any money if you are traveling on a budget. This is because the US dollar is worth more than the Canadian dollar, but you are charged as if they are the same. While most places will warn you of this, not all will.

So, if you spend $50 on groceries, you won't get any change for paying with US dollars even though the current exchange rate is 1 CAN is equal to 0.81 US. This means you would be losing $10 on each $50 purchase and this can quickly add up over time.

Ideally, you should pay with a credit card that doesn't have a foreign transaction fee. If this isn't the case then talk to your current bank/card and if they will automatically convert the transaction so it will show up in the US dollar equivalent on your monthly statement.

The thing to be aware of is the foreign transaction fee; this can be as high as three percent for some debit cards.

BE CAREFUL WHEN PURCHASING FOOD AND WATER

Having a meal plan will save you a lot of money when traveling by RV. The three things that cost the most on RV trips is food, lodging, and gas. Food is one of the items that can easily sneak up on you in cost.

As I've already said, make sure you stock up on groceries in larger towns and make as many of your own meals as possible. Making your own meals really does save a lot of money.

Water is also a surprisingly expensive item in Canada. It can be a good idea to fill your water bottle at any location if they offer free water. You can often find good sources at visitor centers, water fountains, and restrooms.

As long as the water looks okay and is previously disinfected if you are the more cautious type, you can easily save up to five dollars a day on water purchases in Canada.

Keep Track of Your Spending

Lastly, make sure you keep a log of any spending done on your RV trip. This keeps you more accountable for the money you are spending and keeps you in check. RV traveling in Canada and Alaska is an amazing experience, and you don't want to break the bank while traveling.

CONCLUSION

During my many travels, I have rarely found better accommodations and circumstances than those in an RV. There is just something romantic about being able to see all of these natural wonders, creatures, and structures from the comfort of your own transportation. No need to rent a car, hop on overcrowded buses, scramble around trying to find a place to rest if you are already worn out.

You are traveling with a small piece of your home with you wherever you go, which may bring couples, friends, and families closer. One cannot hike something as monumental as a glacier and encounter a whale spewing water at a distance, then not feel closer to the person they experienced this with.

For the more lone travelers, an RV may not be the best option, since it is more difficult to find a place to park something of that scale than it is to find a single bed available for the night somewhere, or a single campsite in a national park.

Needless to say, it is not so much about the method of transportation as it is about the sights you encounter, the people you meet, the foods you consume, and the culture you drench yourself in every time you step out of your vehicle of choice.

An RV is merely a tool, a simple piece in something to make an epic journey all the more convenient and affordable. In order to make a trip work, there has to be a plan of some sort, and a key budget to maintain. Otherwise, it is alarmingly easy for matters to go south, leaving you stranded and tense. Pick a date for your travels, a destination (or destinations in the plural), and an economic goal.

Everything else is a matter of research, maps, schedules, and planning out the little details, so your time is well-spent anywhere you go. So, it is time to put this guide down and plan out that trip you have always wanted to take, but always thought you could not go on because of timely responsibilities.

With realistic goals varying on your family situation and the people who are accompanying you on your trip, you will be able to find a beautiful experience, no matter where you are at.

LAST WORD

I want to say THANK YOU for purchasing and reading this book. I really hope you got a lot out of it!

Can I ask you for a quick favor though?

If you enjoyed this book, I would really appreciate it if you could leave me a Review on Amazon.

I LOVE getting feedback from my wonderful readers, and reviews on Amazon really do make the difference. I read all of my reviews and would love to hear your thoughts.

Thank you so much!!

HELPFUL LINKS & RESOURCES

Best RV forums where you can find out about the latest trends, news and ask questions on any RV related topics.

https://www.tripsavvy.com/best-rv-forums-to-join-2912440

http://www.rvforum.net/joomla/index.php?option=com_content&view=category&layout=blog&id=123&Itemid=104

For RV Buying

www.eBay.com

www.Craigslist.com

www.RVTraders.com

www.CampingWorld.com/RVSales

For RV Price Checking

http://www.nadaguides.com/RVs

https://rvshare.com/blog/rv-values/

https://www.pplmotorhomes.com/kelley-blue-book-rv

Special Driver's License Requirements (If any)

https://www.outdoorsy.com/blog/guide-rv-drivers-licenses-requirements

To learn more about additional RV safety features, you can add to your rig visit here

http://www.livingthervdream.com/RV-safety.html

To find Free Campground in the US, visit these sites

https://ourroaminghearts.com/best-free-camping-sites-usa/

https://www.campendium.com/free-camping

https://www.freshoffthegrid.com/how-to-find-free-camping-usa-canada/

7 Best Smartphone Apps for RV owners (Some are free some are not)

https://www.tripsavvy.com/best-smartphone-apps-for-rv-travel-2912549

Finding Mechanics and Repair Shop while on the road

Try RV forum sites and post or search for mechanics in your immediate area

https://www.rvrepairclub.com/articles/all/

https://www.tripsavvy.com/best-rv-forums-to-join-2912440

For any DIY minor repair, I always find YouTube to be very helpful, so go there and learn how to do many minor repairs all by yourself.

www.YouTube.com

Health Insurance on the Road

http://www.rverinsurance.com/

Made in United States
Troutdale, OR
02/06/2024